SIMPLY DIRAC

SIMPLY DIRAC

HELGE KRAGH

Simply Charly

New York

Simply Charly
5 Columbus Circle, 8th Fl
New York, NY 10019
www.simplycharly.com

ISBN: 978-1-943657-09-4

Contents

Praise for *Simply Dirac*

"Paul Dirac is one of the most influential scientists of the twentieth century, often called 'the theorist's theorist.' Yet he is much less well known than many lesser physicists. In *Simply Dirac*, the distinguished historian Helge Kragh gives an accessible introduction to Dirac's most famous contributions to our understanding of the workings of nature, and gives us a good sense of the theoretician's singular personality. A most enjoyable read."
—**Graham Farmelo, Author of** *The Strangest Man: The Hidden Life of Paul Dirac, Mystic of the Atom*

"Kragh, who is a respected colleague and authoritative historian, has taken up an imposing challenge. Dirac's work is obscured by three barriers to understanding: The complexity of quantum mechanics, the novelty of Dirac's take on this field, and the strangeness of the man. To reveal Dirac's genius through this triple veil in such a clear way was no easy task, but one that Kragh has handled remarkably. He is a reliable guide through this difficult terrain and has contributed many valuable insights to this work."
—**Hans Christian von Baeyer, Chancellor Professor of Physics, Emeritus, at the College of William and Mary**

"What a fantastic entrée into the life of Paul Dirac and the exotic world of Quantum Mechanics, of which he was one of the great pioneers. With its cast of some of the most important scientists of the modern age, this is both an entertaining and an enlightening read."
—**Michael White, Bestselling author of 39 books including** *Isaac Newton: The Last Sorcerer*

"Helge Kragh has crafted an engaging and informative biography of a shy theorist who specialized in difficult physics—a beautiful life in science, in which Paul Dirac's strengths and frailties are treated with a light touch."
—**Simon Mitton, Author of** *Fred Hoyle: A Life in Science*

"Written with depth and clarity, Helge Kragh's *Simply Dirac* is an informative and interesting description of Paul Dirac's work and ideas and of his life and legacy. In particular, I found the author's detailed discussions of methodology, something that is often neglected in a biography as well as his discussion of what little philosophy there was in Dirac's thinking, illuminating."

—**Hans S. Plendl, Professor Emeritus of Physics, Florida State University**

Other *Great Lives* Titles

Simply Austen by Joan Klingel Ray
Simply Beckett by Katherine Weiss
Simply Beethoven by Leon Plantinga
Simply Chaplin by David Sterritt
Simply Chopin by William Smialek
Simply Darwin by Michael Ruse
Simply Descartes by Kurt Smith
Simply Dickens by Paul Schlicke
Simply Dostoevsky by Gary Saul Morson
Simply Edison by Paul Israel
Simply Eliot by Joseph Maddrey
Simply Euler by Robert E. Bradley
Simply Faulkner by Philip Weinstein
Simply Freud by Stephen Frosh
Simply Gödel by Richard Tieszen
Simply Hegel by Robert Wicks
Simply Heidegger by Mahon O'Brien
Simply Hemingway by Mark P. Ott
Simply Hitchcock by David Sterritt
Simply Joyce by Margot Norris
Simply Machiavelli by Robert Fredona
Simply Napoleon by J. David Markham & Matthew Zarzeczny
Simply Newton by Michael Nauenberg
Simply Riemann by Jeremy Gray
Simply Tolstoy by Donna Tussing Orwin
Simply Twain by R. Kent Rasmussen
Simply Wagner by Thomas S. Grey
Simply Wittgenstein by James C. Klagge
Simply Woolf by Mary Ann Caws

Series Editor's Foreword

Simply Charly's "Great Lives" series offers brief but authoritative introductions to the world's most influential people—scientists, artists, writers, economists, and other historical figures whose contributions have had a meaningful and enduring impact on our society. Each book, presented in an engaging and accessible fashion, provides an illuminating look at their works, ideas, personal lives, and the legacies they left behind. Our authors are prominent scholars and other top experts who have dedicated their careers to exploring each facet of their subjects' work and personal lives.

Unlike many other works that are merely descriptions of the major milestones in a person's life, the "Great Lives" series goes above and beyond the standard format and content. Every book includes not just the biographical information, such as the little-known character traits, quirks, strengths and frailties, but, above all, focuses on each individual's extraordinary professional achievements.

In its exploration of famous lives that have sometimes been shrouded in secrecy, surrounded by myths and misconceptions, or caught up in controversies, the "Great Lives" series brings substance, depth, and clarity to the sometimes-complex lives and work of history's most powerful and influential people.

What can a reader learn from the "Great Lives" series? These volumes shed light on the thought processes, as well as specific events and experiences, that led these remarkable people to their groundbreaking discoveries or other achievements; the books also present various challenges they had to face and overcome to make history in their respective fields.

We hope that by exploring this series, readers will not only gain new knowledge and understanding of what drove these geniuses, but also find inspiration for their own lives. Isn't this what a great book is supposed to do?

Charles Carlini, Simply Charly
New York City

Preface

Although not well known to the general public, British physicist Paul Dirac (1902-1984) is indisputably one of the giants of modern science. More specifically, he was one of the founders of quantum mechanics, the theory that, together with Einstein's theory of relativity, defines the modern physical world picture at its most fundamental level. Dirac probably contributed more profoundly to the quantum revolution than any other physicist. His amazing outbursts of scientific brilliance were essentially confined to a decade-long period starting in 1925, after which his creativity and interest in mainstream science declined.

Dirac acquired fame not only for his contributions to physics but also because of his peculiar personality, including such traits as extreme reticence and taciturnity. Social skills were not his strong side. His younger contemporary, Richard Feynman, another quantum genius, was once described as "a second Dirac, only human."

This book offers a condensed account of Dirac's life and science or, more specifically, his life in science. Despite his reserved personality, he was very well connected and during his long career, he interacted with physics luminaries such as Niels Bohr, Werner Heisenberg, J. Robert Oppenheimer, and others. The book is to some extent based on a more detailed and technically demanding monograph I published in 1990, in which one can find further information (*Dirac: A Scientific Biography*, Cambridge University Press). It also includes material from a more recent, and even more, detailed biography by Graham Farmelo (*The Strangest Man*, Faber and Faber).

While Dirac is primarily—and for good reasons—known as the quantum theorist *par excellence*, he also made other noteworthy contributions to the physical sciences. These were not as successful as his early work in quantum theory, but they are nonetheless of considerable interest. I describe in one of the chapters Dirac's unorthodox and highly original cosmological theory, based on the hypothesis that the gravitational constant varies in time—and hence is not a constant. Dirac's cosmology is erroneous but his more general ideas concerning the constants of nature and their possible variation in time are still alive and part of modern physics.

A thorough understanding of Dirac's work requires more than an average expertise in physics and is therefore beyond the reach of most people. However, this should not discourage a curious reader from exploring Dirac's thoughts—it *is* possible to grasp the main ideas of some of his theories without the use of mathematics. This is what I have tried to do. The book requires almost no prior knowledge of mathematics and physics, just an open mind and a little imagination. On the other hand, some basic knowledge of physics and its history is not a disadvantage.

Dirac's life and science can be dealt with in a rather narrow, biographical perspective or a broader, more contextual one. Likewise, it can be dealt with in a strictly chronological order or in a more thematic one. I have chosen the two latter options, which I believe are better suited to explain what made Dirac such an outstanding and remarkably creative physicist. Also, they allow more room for the biographer to point out connections that were scarcely recognized at the time. The book is slim enough to be read from beginning to end in a relatively short time span, allowing the reader to remember the material from one chapter to another. For this reason, I have no qualms about referring in some of the early chapters to topics that will be mentioned only later on in the book.

Although the chapters roughly follow a chronological pattern, a few of them cover much of Dirac's life—and some beyond it—focusing on themes that were not time-sensitive or specific to a particular scientific work. Some parts of a scientist's work, as well as its historical significance within a broader context, can only be properly evaluated with the passage of time.

As I did in my 1990 monograph, here too I have chosen to pay attention to aspects of a more general, methodological, and philosophical nature. Dirac was not a philosopher, but one does not need to dig deeply into his work to find assumptions and guiding themes that can best be characterized as philosophical. The most original of these themes and the one he felt most committed to was the so-called "principle of mathematical beauty." It is more than a little surprising that the emotionally restricted Dirac, an almost inhuman worshiper of rationality and logic in science as well as in life, should develop such a strong commitment to the nebulous concept of beauty. He seriously believed that a theory of great mathematical aesthetic should be preferred over a less beautiful rival theory, even if the latter were empirically superior. But isn't beauty in the eye of the beholder?

Helge Kragh
Copenhagen, Denmark

1

Strangeness and Genius

A t the turn of the millennium in the year 2000, a senior Italian physicist reflected on which individual had had the greatest influence on 20th-century physics. "Paul Dirac had a much bigger impact on modern science in the 20th century than Albert Einstein," he concluded. Paul Dirac? Who was he? While Einstein is the undisputed icon of modern theoretical physics, Dirac is little known outside the physics community, certainly less so than Niels Bohr, Werner Heisenberg, Erwin Schrödinger, and Richard Feynman. And yet, Dirac unquestionably was a creative physicist of the same elevated rank, and his relative anonymity is unwarranted. For one, Einstein recognized his genius early on. While trying, in 1926, to understand a paper by the then 24-year-old British physicist who, at the time, was unknown to him, Einstein wrote in a letter, almost in despair: "I have trouble with Dirac. This balancing on the dizzying path between genius and madness is awful."

Paul Adrien Maurice Dirac—for that was his full name—was a late prodigy. Born on August 8, 1902, in Bristol, the second child of Charles Dirac and Florence née Holten, Paul had two siblings: an older brother Reginald (who committed suicide at 24) and a younger sister, Beatrice. His father was a French-speaking Swiss immigrant who had settled in Bristol around 1890 and, for this reason, Paul was registered as Swiss by birth. Only in 1919, when he was 17 years old, did he acquire British nationality. The family lived in a small house on 15 Monk Road in suburban Bristol, a location unlikely to attract tourists. Today, a plaque informs passers-by of the building's erstwhile occupant: "Nobel Prize Laureate in 1933 who revealed the secrets of quantum physics and antimatter." In 1913, the Dirac family moved to a bigger and more expensive home at 6 Julius Road in another part of Bristol.

Paul had a rather unhappy childhood and youth, primarily the result of his authoritarian father's distaste for social contacts (a trait that the elder Dirac passed on to his son). A highly regarded teacher, Charles recognized Paul's unusual abilities and encouraged his education. On the other hand, he also dominated his family and kept his children in a virtual prison as far as emotional and social life was concerned. They were brought up in a crippling atmosphere of cold, silence and isolation. "I had no social life at all as a child," Paul once recalled. As a young man, he never had a girlfriend—or any other friend for that matter. When he finally broke out of that "prison" and left Bristol, he started to hate his father and avoided him if at all possible. Most likely, Paul's reserved and solitary nature was a product of his childhood.

In 1918, Paul entered Bristol University as a student of electrical engineering; he graduated three years later with top honors. Unable to find a job, he was lucky to get accepted as a student of mathematics at the same university. He was more interested in mathematics than engineering anyhow. Finally, in the fall of 1923, a new chapter in his life started as he left Bristol to enroll as a research student at Cambridge's St. John's College.

Relativity and quantum theory were not subjects that Dirac was taught at Bristol University. "We were studying engineering, and all of our work was based on Newton," he said in 1979 at a conference celebrating the centenary of Einstein's birth. "We had absolute faith in Newton, and now we learned that Newton was wrong in some mysterious way." When Dirac arrived in Cambridge, he was already thoroughly acquainted with Einstein's theory of relativity.

In 1919, British astronomers Arthur Eddington and Frank Dyson had confirmed from observations of a solar eclipse that starlight would bend around the Sun in agreement with the general theory of relativity. This meant that Einstein was right and Newton wrong. After this confirmation of Einstein's theory, relativity was on everybody's lips. Dirac was no exception. "We discussed it very much," he recalled. "Relativity was a subject that everybody felt himself competent to write about in a general philosophical way. The philosophers just put forward the view that everything had to be considered relatively to something else, and they rather claimed that they had known about relativity all along." Dirac took a course on relativity theory and scientific thought given by the Bristol philosopher Charlie Broad and later followed up on it by self-studies of the mathematical content of Einstein's theory. Thirty years later, Broad remembered that Dirac had attended his lectures. He described him as "one whose shoe-laces I was not worthy to unloose." When Dirac came to Cambridge, he had mastered the essentials of both the special and general theory of relativity, including much of the abstract mathematical apparatus underlying the theories. Relativity was Dirac's first love, but it was quantum theory that made his fortune.

As a research student in Cambridge, Dirac lived a quiet life, confining himself entirely to scientific studies and taking almost no part in social activities. One of his fellow research students was the American John Slater, who would soon emerge as a leader of quantum physics and its applications in chemistry. Characteristically, Dirac and Slater never talked together and only realized years later that they had followed some of the same courses. Still, as Dirac met more people, he gradually became a little less shy and introverted, as shown by his membership in 1924 in two academic clubs for mathematicians and physicists—the $\nabla^2 V$ (del-squared V) Club and the Kapitza Club. The latter was an informal discussion group founded by and named after the Russian physicist Peter Kapitza.

Dirac was fortunate to be assigned Ralph Fowler as his supervisor—not because Fowler was very active in supervising him but because he was one of the very few British physicists with expert knowledge of atomic and quantum theory. The quantum theory of atomic structure was effectively founded by Niels Bohr in 1913 when he applied Max Planck's idea of discrete energy quanta to explain the structure of atoms. Apart from Bohr and his school in Copenhagen, the theory was dominated by German physicists from the universities of Göttingen and Munich. On the other hand, British physicists generally resisted or ignored the new theory.

In the early 1920s, the semi-classical quantum theory based on Bohr's planetary model of the atom encountered an increasing number of difficulties. It pictured the atom as a system of electrons revolving in definite orbits around the nucleus, not unlike the planets in our solar system. Although the theory was in many respects successful, physicists working with it realized that there was something seriously wrong. They thought that perhaps the very notion of electron orbits, a remnant of classical theory, ought to be abandoned. Unfortunately, neither Bohr nor his colleagues in Germany had a better alternative. It was in these circumstances that Dirac was first exposed to quantum theory. Guided by Fowler, he soon mastered the intricacies of quantum atomic theory, subsequently writing a couple of papers on this topic. In the summer of 1925, less than two years after he had arrived in Cambridge, he had published six papers on theoretical physics.

Although an impressive record, none of the papers was strikingly original.

In 1927, only a year after he had completed his Ph.D. at Cambridge University, Dirac was invited to participate in the prestigious Solvay conference in Brussels, which focused on the physical meaning of the new quantum mechanics and featured a soon-to-be-famous dialogue between Einstein and Bohr. The following year, Dirac was offered the professorship in applied mathematics at Manchester University but turned down the offer. Then, in 1930, he was elected Fellow of the Royal Society, one of the youngest Fellows ever in the history of the distinguished academy founded in 1662. And in 1932, he was appointed Lucasian professor of mathematics at Cambridge, the chair once occupied by Isaac Newton. The name of the chair derives from Henry Lucas, a Cambridge member of the British parliament who founded it in 1663.

Dirac in 1938. Credit: Niels Bohr Archive, Copenhagen.

The culmination of Dirac's scientific career came in November 1933 when he had been awarded the Nobel Prize in physics, sharing it with Schrödinger. One would imagine that young Dirac was overjoyed to become a Nobel laureate, but this was not the case. In fact, at first, he seriously contemplated rejecting the prize because of the publicity it would inevitably bring with it. But as the British physicist Ernest Rutherford pointed out to him, a refusal would surely create much more publicity, so Dirac reluctantly accepted it. At the time, a London newspaper, the *Sunday Dispatch*, described the 31-year-old Cambridge professor to be "as shy as a gazelle and as modest as a Victorian maid." It added that he "fears all women."

By the way, when Dirac arrived in Stockholm to receive the prize and deliver the traditional Nobel lecture in front of the Swedish king, he brought his mother with him. According to the rules of the Nobel Foundation, he was permitted to invite one guest, and he deliberately chose not to ask his father, which is not surprising, considering the ill feeling Dirac had harbored towards Charles.

Nobel Prize winners have the right to nominate scientists within their field for future prizes. Most laureates take advantage of this right, realizing that the award is an important instrument of international science policy. Dirac was not interested in science policy, but he did use his right in 1946 and again in 1950 to nominate his friend Peter Kapitza. Dirac met Kapitza when both worked in Cambridge, from about 1921 to 1934, and also knew him from his many travels in Russia. Although Dirac's two nominations were unsuccessful, in 1978 Kapitza finally received the Nobel Prize for his significant contributions to low-temperature physics. He was 84 years old.

There is a concept in elementary particle physics called "strangeness," a kind of quantum number that characterizes a rapidly decaying particle. While the proton and the electron are not strange particles, more exotic elementary particles are ascribed a strangeness number different from zero. For example, the omega-minus particle consisting of three quarks has strangeness − 3, which makes it a very strange particle indeed. Had Dirac been an elementary particle, he definitely would be classified as strange, perhaps even stranger than omega-minus. A major biography of Dirac published in 2009 carries the title *The Strangest Man*. This is undoubtedly an exaggeration, but Dirac's personality was in some ways peculiar and eccentric, exhibiting character traits that went back to his childhood and can well be described as strange. One of these traits, as illustrated in the case of the Nobel Prize, was his dislike of honors and publicity of any kind. In 1953, for example, he turned down a knighthood, mainly because he did not want to be addressed as "Sir Paul." Of the few honors that he did accept, the most prestigious was the Order of Merit, which he received in 1973 (and which did not require any change of name). Dirac also received numerous offers of honorary doctorates but invariably declined them all. In a letter to his friend, the American physicist and later Nobel laureate John Van Vleck, he wrote, "I like conferences and lectures less and less as I get older, and I never did like celebrations."

Dirac's reticence and taciturn nature were legendary. He was antisocial and rarely spoke spontaneously, preferring to use as few words as possible. A Cambridge physicist who had known Dirac for many years once told of how Dirac typically responded when asked a scientific question: "He looks for five minutes at the ceiling, five minutes at the windows, and then says 'Yes' or 'No.' And he is always right." Other sources claimed that Dirac's vocabulary was larger, consisting of five and not just two words, for he frequently responded with "I don't know." Another of Dirac's colleagues described him as a "total rationalist," citing Dirac's idiosyncratic and exaggerated insistence on logic, as well as intellectual and verbal economy. He would answer a direct question but not address a comment or statement that, from a logical point of view, did not demand a response. According to one anecdote, after Dirac had delivered a lecture, a student in the audience said that he did not understand a formula. Nothing happened, no sign of reaction from the lecturer. After some time of embarrassing silence, Dirac was requested to answer the question. "It is not a question, it is a statement," he tersely responded.

While other great scientists have sometimes been interested in and inspired by philosophy, literature, music and political ideas, these aspects of intellectual life were largely absent in Dirac's universe. In his younger and intensely creative days he focused one-sidedly on theoretical physics, which completely absorbed his mind. He was close to being a monomaniac. To a Swedish newspaper, interviewing him on the occasion of his Nobel Prize, he said: "I am not interested in literature, I do not go to the theatre, and I do not listen to music. I am occupied with atomic theories."

When Dirac became aware of the American physicist J. Robert Oppenheimer's interest in poetry and Buddhist philosophy, he was deeply puzzled. "How can you do physics and poetry at the same time?" he asked. "The aim of science is to make difficult things understandable in a simpler way; the aim of poetry is to state simple things in an incomprehensible way. The two are incompatible." Once, Kapitza gave Dirac an English translation of Dostoyevsky's *Crime and Punishment* and asked him to read it. Later, when Kapitza asked if he had enjoyed the book, Dirac's only comment was: "It is nice, but in one of the chapters the author made a mistake. He describes the Sun as rising twice on the same day."

In 1926, Dirac spent a term at Bohr's Institute in Copenhagen, where he became closely acquainted with the Danish atomic physicist and quantum sage. "We had long talks together," he recalled, "long talks on which Bohr did practically all the talking." Bohr was intrigued by the personality of the young Englishman, whom he characterized as a strange yet "complete logical genius."

Bohr was in most respects very different from Dirac—socially, culturally, and regarding his scientific style. Yet, Dirac admired his colleague and characterized him as the deepest thinker he had ever met. In a 1933 letter to Bohr, Dirac wrote: "I feel that all my deepest ideas have been very greatly and favourably influenced by the talks I have had with you, more than with anyone else." He later said that Bohr occupied the same position regarding atomic theory as Newton did concerning classical mechanics.

While in Copenhagen, Dirac became for the first time part of a vibrant scientific environment based on collaboration and group discussion. On Bohr's invitation, he even spent Christmas with Bohr and his family. The stay in Copenhagen was a change in Dirac's life, but not even the friendly atmosphere at Bohr's institute could break his solitary habits and deep-rooted preference for isolation.

While Bohr's creativity was boosted by long conversations with assistants and colleagues, and his publications went through a tortuous process with numerous draft versions, Dirac's way of working was completely different. His mother had taught him to think first and then write—advice Dirac took to heart. When writing a manuscript, he would first draw up the whole work in his mind. Only then would he write it down in his meticulous handwriting, and this first draft would need few, if any, corrections. One of the students at Bohr's institute recalled that Dirac appeared "almost mysterious" as he sat alone in the innermost room of the library. He "was so absorbed in his thoughts that we hardly dared to creep into the room, afraid as we were to disturb him. He could spend a whole day in the same position, writing an entire article, slowly and without ever crossing anything out."

2

Quantum Wizard

U nknown to Dirac, in the summer of 1925 Werner Heisenberg had figured out the skeleton of a new and abstract "quantum mechanics" that promised to be fundamental, logically consistent, and not plagued by the difficulties of the existing quantum theory of atomic structure. Only eight months older than Dirac, Heisenberg was a graduate student of Max Born in Göttingen. Like Dirac, he had not yet obtained his Ph.D. degree.

The young German reasoned that a truly fundamental theory had to contain observable quantities only. By this criterion, electron orbits were no longer legitimate, whereas the frequencies of light emitted by atoms were. After all, who had ever observed an electron orbiting around a nucleus? Transforming this general idea into an abstract mathematical scheme, Heisenberg expressed physical quantities by arrays of symbols soon recognized to be matrices. One of the arrays might represent the position of an electron (Q) and another array its momentum (P, which equals mass times velocity). Heisenberg's theory led to a mysterious law of multiplication according to which QP differed from PQ, that is, $QP \neq PQ$. It was as if 3×2 was not always equal to 2×3, or that the two numbers do not "commute." Noting the puzzling fact that in general physical quantities did not commute, Heisenberg, at first, thought it was a flaw in his theory that might disappear when it was further developed.

Heisenberg's seminal paper was published in a German journal on September 18, 1925, but Dirac knew of it ahead of publication. In August, Heisenberg had sent proofs of his forthcoming paper to Ralph Fowler, who sent them on to Dirac with a note saying, "What do you think of this? I shall be glad to hear." Dirac first thought that it was of no interest, but a closer study told him a different story. He now realized that far from being a flaw, the strange appearance of non-commuting physical variables was the key element in the new mechanics and, consequently, had to be understood. Some versions of classical mechanics, he remembered, operated with non-commuting variables, which indicated that Heisenberg's idea might be expressed in formal analogy with classical theory. The crucial insight came to Dirac "in a flash" (as he recalled) one afternoon at the beginning of October. A couple of weeks later he had a paper ready with the ambitious title "The Fundamental Equations of Quantum Mechanics." This was the first paper that mentioned the term "quantum mechanics" in its title and with a meaning recognizable by modern physicists.

Among the fundamental equations was a significant sharpening of Heisenberg's non-commuting variables. PQ and QP did not only differ, but, according to Dirac, they differed by a precise amount given by the tiny constant of nature Max Planck had introduced in 1900: $PQ - QP \sim h$. Planck's constant is tiny indeed ($h = 6.6 \times 10^{-34}$ in units of joule × second), which explains why position and momentum commute for a canon-ball but not for an electron. Dirac's paper also contained a quantum analogue of the classical equation of motion, that is, an expression of how a physical quantity varies in time. Without an equation of motion, quantum mechanics would not be of much value, just as classical mechanics would be of little use without Newton's second law of motion.

Even back in the 1920s, physics was a very competitive field (as it remains to this day). Dirac was aware that he was in competition with the German physicists, but the question of priority of the laws of quantum mechanics was not of great concern to him. Yet, he must have been disappointed when Heisenberg informed him in a letter of November 20 that most of the results in Dirac's "extraordinarily beautiful paper" had already been derived by Born and another talented young Göttingen physicist, Pascual Jordan. The two Germans had extended and clarified Heisenberg's theory, recognizing for the first time that it could be formulated in the language of matrix calculus. Consequently, the Göttingen approach to quantum mechanics was often referred to as "matrix mechanics." In a lengthy follow-up paper known as the *Dreimännerarbeit* ("three-man paper") Born, Heisenberg, and Jordan further developed matrix mechanics into what today is considered to be the first full exposition of quantum mechanics.

Dirac followed the development in Germany with interest but decided to pursue his own ideas. On their side, the German physicists were quick to appreciate the surprising progress made in Cambridge by the "Englishman working with Fowler"—this is how Heisenberg referred to Dirac in a letter of November 24 to his Austrian colleague Wolfgang Pauli. And this is what Born recalled: "The name Dirac was completely unknown to me. The author appeared to be a youngster, yet everything was perfect in its way and admirable." The German-speaking physicists were not used to competition and especially not from their British counterparts.

The version of quantum mechanics that Dirac developed in 1926 was known as "q-number algebra," indicating that it was essentially a mathematical theory that could be applied to problems of physics. Measurable properties are given by numbers read on an instrument—for instance, the weight of a body as read on a balance. They are ordinary or classical numbers that satisfy the law of commutation (3×2 *is* equal to 2×3). Quantum variables, on the other hand, do not satisfy the law. They are members of a new class of q-numbers with mathematical properties of its own. Q-numbers are queer. On this basis, Dirac established his abstract q-number algebraic theory. Given the theory's thoroughly algebraic and unvisualizable character, it is remarkable that it may have been inspired by geometric considerations. Dirac later said that while he published in the algebraic style, he thought in terms of pictures and diagrams. "I prefer the relationships which I can visualize in geometric terms," he noted.

Despite its apparent remoteness from physical reality, Dirac's theory turned out to be equivalent to the matrix mechanics of the German physicists, and, as such, described the quantum world of atoms, molecules, and light. For example, Dirac succeeded in explaining the spectrum of hydrogen in accordance with Bohr's old atomic theory. Symptomatic of the competitiveness of the period, Pauli did the same, using more cumbersome methods of matrix mechanics.

In early 1926, there were basically two versions of quantum mechanics, the Göttingen matrix mechanics, and Dirac's q-number theory. The latter was very much Dirac's own and rarely used by other physicists. When the Austrian physicist Erwin Schrödinger published his new "wave mechanics" a few months later, the number of versions grew to three. For a while, confusion increased as Schrödinger's theory was quite different from the abstract schemes developed in Göttingen and Cambridge. It described particles and atomic phenomena in terms of a continuous wave function (ψ), which satisfied a classical-looking equation of motion soon known as the Schrödinger equation. The physical meaning of the wave function was a matter of some dispute until Born suggested the currently accepted interpretation, namely, that ψ is a measure of the *probability* of something happening. Dirac, at first, resented the new wave mechanics, which he thought was formulated in a too classical framework. "I definitely had a hostility to

Schrödinger's ideas," he recalled. However, the hostility did not last long. When it was proved that wave mechanics was mathematically equivalent to matrix mechanics (and also to q-number algebra), Dirac adopted a more pragmatic attitude, often mixing elements of his own theory with those of Schrödinger's.

As a result of his study of Schrödinger's theory, in August of 1926 Dirac published an important paper in which he clarified the physical meaning of the mysterious ψ-function and used a generalized version of the Schrödinger equation to solve problems of physics. The most important result was a fundamental distinction between two classes of particles on the basis of their different wave functions. Some particles, such as electrons and protons, were characterized by "anti-symmetrical" wave functions, while other particles, including the light quantum or photon, could be described by "symmetrical" wave functions. The quantum behavior of the first class of particles was initially examined by the Italian physicist Enrico Fermi; they became known as Fermi-Dirac particles (contrary to the photon, which is a Bose-Einstein particle). Later, Dirac invented the more convenient names *fermion* and *boson* for the two kinds of particles—designations that have long been part of physicists' general vocabulary. The latter name is a reference to the Indian physicist Satyendra Nath Bose whose idea was improved by Einstein. As Pauli later proved, all fermions have half-integral spin (½ for an electron) and all bosons feature integral spin (0 for a photon).

Dirac's paper of August 1926 was widely recognized to be an important contribution to quantum mechanics, but also one that was very hard to understand. It had to be deciphered, line by line. Einstein was not the only one who had troubles with Dirac's abstract and condensed style of writing. In an October 1926 letter to Bohr, Schrödinger expressed his admiration for Dirac's paper, adding, however, that there was much in it he found difficult to comprehend: "Dirac has a completely original and unique method of thinking, which—precisely for this reason—will yield the most valuable results, hidden to the rest of us," he wrote. "But he has no idea how *difficult* his papers are for the normal human being."

At the time when Bohr read the letter, Dirac stayed with him in Copenhagen, the first of his many journeys abroad. In May of 1926, he had completed his Ph.D. in Cambridge. The title of his doctoral dissertation was as simple as it was concise—just "Quantum Mechanics," the first one ever written on the subject. Even before he was granted the doctoral degree, Dirac gave the first course in quantum mechanics taught at a British university. Among the few students who attended was J. Robert Oppenheimer, who was on his way to a distinguished career in physics. During and after World War II, he became a public figure, a result of his appointment as scientific director of the Manhattan Project established to construct the atomic bomb. While Dirac and Oppenheimer hardly knew each other at Cambridge, when they met again in Göttingen the following year, they developed a lasting friendship.

The stay in Copenhagen was immensely fruitful for Dirac, as was his subsequent visit to Göttingen. In the fall of 1926, quantum mechanics had made huge progress. However, a general and unified formalism associated with a conceptual clarification was still missing. It was this excessively difficult task that Dirac addressed in Copenhagen. The result of his intellectual efforts, a fundamental paper on "The Physical Interpretation of the Quantum Dynamics," was completed in early December. Unknown to Dirac, Jordan was working on the same problem in Göttingen and arrived independently at a theory of the same generality and grandiose scope. Dirac's paper was a mathematical and conceptual *tour de force* based on strictly logical deductions, a procedure which appealed to his rational mind. "This work," he recalled, "gave me more pleasure in carrying it through than any of the other papers which I have written on quantum mechanics either before or after."

At the time, Born had shown that Schrödinger's ψ–function could not itself be ascribed a definite physical meaning, in the sense that it was not measurable, but that the square of the function determined a probability density. For example, there is a certain probability that an electron at a time will be located in a volume element dV and this probability is given by $\psi^2 dV$. Dirac's general theory comprised Born's probabilistic interpretation of quantum mechanics without introducing the interpretation as an axiom. Another characteristic feature of quantum mechanics is the impossibility of knowing the exact location of a particle and the exact value of its momentum simultaneously. This surprising result, so foreign to the determinism inherent in classical mechanics, was first announced by Heisenberg in a classic paper published in May 1927. According to Heisenberg's principle of uncertainty or indeterminacy, in any measurement, there is a minimum indeterminacy Δq in the position of a particle, and similarly a minimum indeterminacy Δp in its momentum. Each of the uncertainties can be zero, but not both at the same time. They are bound together by the relation $\Delta q \Delta p \sim h$, which can be seen as an instance of the lack of commutativity of q and p.

In his Copenhagen paper, Dirac came close to formulating Heisenberg's deep insight and its consequence that determinism is ruled out in the quantum world: "One can suppose that the initial state of a system determines definitely the state of the system at any subsequent time. If, however, one describes the state of the system at an arbitrary time by giving numerical values to the co-ordinates and momenta, then one cannot actually set up a one–one correspondence between the values of these co-ordinates and momenta initially and their values at a subsequent time." Although close to the uncertainty relations in December 1926, Dirac felt no need to formulate his insight into a general principle concerning the limitation of measurements.

Another result of Dirac's paper, a mathematical innovation, merits attention. To facilitate some of his calculations and state them in a more condensed way, he introduced a function $\delta(x)$ with the strange property that it is equal to zero for all values of x except at $x = 0$, where $\delta(0)$ equals infinity. The area covered by this function is neither zero nor infinity, as one might perhaps expect, but exactly one. Dirac was not really the first to make use of a wildly discontinuous function of this kind, but it was only with his work that it became a powerful tool in quantum mechanics and other areas of theoretical physics. It is not, strictly speaking, a "function," but what mathematicians call a "distribution." Dirac was not obsessed by mathematical rigor, and he introduced his delta-function without caring much about whether or not it was justified by the mathematicians' standards. What mattered to him was that it was useful from the point of view of physics.

The strange delta-function was eventually justified in the sense that it became part of the general and mathematically rigorous theory of distributions. It is common to see Dirac's delta-function as a gift from the physicists to the mathematicians, but the actual connection between Dirac's innovation and the theory of distributions was tenuous. The mathematical distribution theory was invented in 1944 by the French mathematician Laurent Schwartz, who earlier had come across Dirac's formulae involving the delta-function. However, he found them "so crazy from a mathematical point of view that there was simply no question of accepting them." Schwartz's invention was not motivated by physics but by problems in pure mathematics. As he later commented: "It's a good thing that theoretical physicists do not wait for mathematical justification before going ahead with their theories!" Schwartz and Dirac came to know each other in 1949 when both lectured at a mathematical seminar in Vancouver.

Many people would have rested on their laurels, at least for a while, after having completed work so demanding as the paper on the physical interpretation of quantum mechanics. But not Dirac. On the contrary, he continued straight ahead with another important work, in which he applied quantum mechanics to the electromagnetic field making up the waves of light. Although attempts at a quantum electrodynamics (as the theory is called) had previously been made in 1925 by Jordan in the *Dreimännerarbeit*, it was only with Dirac's new paper on the interaction of matter and radiation that a proper foundation of quantum electrodynamics was laid. His theory dealt with emission and absorption of light waves or photons, which to Dirac were just two names for the same thing—the one depicting light as waves and the other as particles. He was pleased to note that his theory contained "a complete harmony between the wave and light-quantum descriptions."

Instead of treating the characteristic quantities of the radiation field as ordinary c-numbers, he now treated them as q-numbers or quantum variables, which is the essence of so-called "second quantization." This important idea goes back to Dirac's work published in 1927. It enabled him to calculate the probabilities of emission, absorption, and scattering of light in agreement with experimental knowledge and previous theoretical formulae. In addition, he could explain dispersion, the phenomenon where light changes its wavelength after having passed matter. Yet Dirac was not entirely satisfied, as he had merely justified on the basis of quantum mechanics what was already known. Referring to second quantization, he remarked at the end of his life, "It was a bit of disappointment to find that nothing really new came out of the idea." Important as Dirac's radiation theory was, it was restricted to particles satisfying Bose-Einstein statistics (bosons), which in practice meant light in the form of photons. At the time, Dirac did not attempt to extend his theory to cover also fermions such as electrons. It was left to Jordan and other physicists in the German tradition to generalize the method of second quantization in such a way that it was applicable to electrons and other particles carrying mass.

Between February and June of 1927, Dirac stayed in Göttingen, which was the center of theoretical physics even more than Copenhagen. There, he met not only the German quantum theorists, including Born, Jordan, and Heisenberg, but also many visiting foreigners. One of them was the American physicist Raymond Birge, who in a letter to a colleague in the United States reported on the impression Dirac made in the German university town: "When he talks, Born just sits and listens to him open-mouthed. That Dirac thinks of absolutely nothing but physics." The Russian Igor Tamm, a later Nobel laureate, was another visiting physicist greatly impressed by Dirac. Back in Moscow, Tamm wrote in a letter to a relative about his unforgettable meeting with this "true man of genius," whom he had had the privilege of befriending. "Do not smile that it sounds high-flown; I really mean it. I know that when I grow old I'll be telling my grandchildren with pride about that acquaintance of mine."

On his way back to Cambridge, Dirac visited another of the continental centers of quantum physics, the University of Leiden in the Netherlands. He was invited by Paul Ehrenfest, who was a close friend of Bohr and had done important work in both the old and the new quantum theory. Ehrenfest had recognized Dirac's genius at an early stage and was eager to know more of his methods. Shortly before Dirac arrived in Leiden, Ehrenfest wrote to him, in much the same vein as Schrödinger and Einstein had previously: "We spent many, many hours going over a few pages of your work before we understood them! And many points are still as dark to us as the most moonless night!"

In the late 1920s, physicists discussed not only the physical meaning of quantum mechanics, but also its broader philosophical implications. Although the two questions were intimately connected, Dirac felt much more at home on the first question than the second one. Basically, he was not very interested in the interpretation debate in so far that it was unrelated to the equations of quantum mechanics. For example, he disliked Bohr's complementarity principle, a broadly formulated interpretation of the quantum world and its relation to the classical world that Bohr had suggested in 1927. Dirac felt that it involved too much philosophy and too little physics. "It doesn't provide you with any equations which you didn't have before," was his reason for dismissing Bohr's principle.

But Dirac could not avoid the issue of interpretation such as it came up in the discussions between Bohr, Einstein, Heisenberg, Schrödinger, and others. Although he differed in some respects from the Bohr-Heisenberg view known as the Copenhagen interpretation, on the whole, he accepted that quantum mechanics was not a theory of nature but solely a way of calculating and predicting measurable quantities. Born paraphrased Dirac's view, or what he called his *l'art pour l'art* attitude, as follows: "The existence of a mathematically consistent theory is all we want. It represents everything that can be said about the empirical world; we can predict with its help unobserved phenomena, and that is all we wish. What you mean by an objective world we don't know and don't care."

Dirac believed that getting the right equations was more important than discussing questions of interpretation, which, in the end, might be a matter of opinion rather than fact. On the other hand, he was neither uninformed about nor uninterested in the interpretation issue. As a participant in the famous 1927 Solvay conference in Brussels, he witnessed the epic debate between Bohr and Einstein, but without taking much part in the discussion. As he explained it, "I listened to their arguments, but I did not join in them, essentially because I was not very much interested. I was more interested in getting the correct equations." However, he did give a fairly elaborate exposition of his own view, which was critically discussed by Born and Heisenberg. While Heisenberg tended to conceive of nature as the product of the observer's free will, Dirac suggested the much less subjectivist view that it was nature itself that determined the outcome of an experiment. Of course, he added, only human observers could decide what kind of experiment to make.

Two years after the Solvay Conference, Dirac was approached on behalf of Oxford University Press by James G. Crowther, a science journalist and author, who wanted him to write a textbook on quantum mechanics. Crowther recalled that Dirac "was living in a simply furnished attic in St. John's College. He had a wooden desk of the kind that is used in schools. He was seated at this apparently writing the great work straight off." The result of this meeting was *Principles of Quantum Mechanics* (1930), probably the most important textbook on the subject ever published, and a rich source for understanding Dirac's view of quantum physics. Dirac clearly had an agenda in writing the book, namely to disseminate what *he* thought were the basic principles and proper methods of quantum mechanics. He wanted to shape a theory, which had not yet found its final form.

Principles did much to disseminate views of the Copenhagen school to a generation of young physicists. In agreement with Bohr, in the preface Dirac called attention to "the increasing recognition of the part played by the observer himself in introducing the regularities that appear in his observations." This he considered "very satisfactory from a philosophical point of view." Dirac further pointed out that the

THE

PRINCIPLES

OF

QUANTUM MECHANICS

BY

P. A. M. DIRAC

FELLOW OF ST. JOHN'S COLLEGE
CAMBRIDGE

SECOND EDITION

OXFORD
AT THE CLARENDON PRESS
1935

The second edition of Dirac's famous textbook.

fundamental laws of nature "do not govern the world as it appears in our mental picture in any very direct way, but instead they control a substratum of which we cannot form a mental picture without introducing irrelevancies." From the beginning to the end, *Principles* was based on what he called the "symbolic method." Dirac wanted to present the general theory of quantum mechanics in a way that was free of physical interpretation. The symbols, he said, were used "in an abstract way, the algebraic axioms that they satisfy and the connection between equations involving them and physical conditions being all that is required."

Compared with other textbooks in theoretical physics,—or textbooks of any kind—*Principles* was unusual. With no illustrations, no index, and almost no references, it was not a reader-friendly work. Nor had Dirac found it necessary to add the customary list with suggestions for further reading. The book was also completely ahistorical, presenting its subject as if it were an abstract mathematical discipline coming down from the heavens. Experiments were given very low priority. By ordinary pedagogical standards, it was simply a catastrophe, but pedagogy was obviously not what interested Dirac most. The exposition was highly original. While all other textbooks introduce Planck's constant early on, it only appeared on page 95 of the book's 264 pages. Similarly, readers had to wait until page 104 to meet the Schrödinger equation. This was fully intentional, a consequence of the symbolic method.

Despite its obvious pedagogical deficiencies, *Principles* became a great success. The first English edition sold about 2,000 copies and the German and Russian translations sold even more. The book quickly established itself as the standard work on quantum mechanics, used not only by students as a textbook, but also by many experienced research physicists. It was widely reviewed in the physics journals, in almost all cases positively and in some even enthusiastically. It was a common feature of the reviews to praise the book for its directness, generality, and completeness. According to Oppenheimer, it was "astonishingly complete" and "unitary and coherent." He observed that *Principles* was "clear, with a clarity dangerous for the beginner, deductive, and in its foundation abstract" and also that "the virtual contact with experiment is made quite late in the book." However, in spite of all its qualities, Oppenheimer added a warning: "The book remains a difficult book, and one suited only to those who come to it with some familiarity with the theory. It should not be the sole text, nor the first text, in quantum theory." Ehrenfest had more than just some familiarity with quantum theory but nonetheless found *Principles* a hard read. "A terrible book—you can't tear it apart!" is how he is said to have reacted.

Philosophically minded reviewers preferred to interpret Dirac's textbook in accordance with their own philosophical tastes. Eddington, at the time Britain's best-known scientist and popular writer of science, favored a philosophical view of science that could be described as a hybrid of rationalism and idealism. He was fascinated by Dirac's approach to physics in general and his wave equation of the electron in particular. Eddington praised Dirac's symbolic version of quantum mechanics as "highly transcendental, almost mystical" and found that it agreed with his own view of the universe as a dematerialized world of shadows dressed up in mathematical symbols. Dirac was probably surprised, not knowing that he was almost a mystic. The Austrian physicist and philosopher Philipp Frank, professor in Prague and a leading figure in the school of logical positivism, read *Principles* as indirect support of positivist philosophy. He was pleased with what he saw as Dirac's philosophical position, namely, that physical theory can only answer questions that relate to the outcome of experiments, whether real or imagined. Frank was a close friend of Einstein, who was no less impressed by Dirac's book. Referring to the standard probabilistic interpretation of quantum mechanics (which Einstein did not accept) he wrote that it was to Dirac "to whom, in my opinion, we owe the most logically perfect presentation of this theory."

3

Anti-Worlds

With his fundamental papers published between 1925 and 1927, Dirac had proved himself a quantum wizard, a leading physicist of the quantum-mechanical revolution. However, although his contributions were invariably original and recognized to be highly significant, in almost all cases other European physicists obtained the same results—and in some cases, they even scooped him. Dirac felt that he still lived in Heisenberg's shadow and had not yet produced a deep and really novel theory. The Nobel Committee in Stockholm even concluded that "Dirac is in the front rank of the group of researchers who have set themselves the task to realize Heisenberg's bold thought," but noted that "Dirac is a successor in relation to Heisenberg."

The deep and really novel theory that he dreamed of came unexpectedly to him at the end of 1927. The eponymous Dirac equation is no less fundamental than the better-known Schrödinger equation, and its consequences even more amazing. The memorial stone for Dirac at Westminster Abbey reproduces the equation in a compact form familiar to modern physicists: $i\gamma\partial\psi = m\psi$. (Appropriately, the stone is placed near the tomb of Isaac Newton). To understand the origin and significance of this mysteriously-looking equation we need to go back to the spring of 1926.

When Schrödinger introduced his wave equation to the world of physics, he used it to calculate the energy levels of the hydrogen atom and derive the same spectral lines that Bohr had obtained from the old quantum theory in 1913. The hydrogen spectrum was a triumph of wave mechanics, but Schrödinger realized that the triumph was incomplete: the spectral lines were not sharp but consisted of narrowly spaced doublets, a phenomenon known as "fine structure." The separation of the doublet lines, as given by the difference in frequency, is very small and can be expressed by a number known as the fine-structure constant. This number would play an important role in

Dirac's physics. Within the framework of the Bohr model, the fine structure could be accounted for by taking into regard the theory of relativity, but by 1926 Bohr's orbital model was dead. Schrödinger was acutely aware that his equation did not satisfy the requirements of relativity and, probably, for this reason, was unable to explain hydrogen's fine structure.

The Schrödinger wave equation contains terms that correspond to a particle's energy E and its momentum p. According to relativity theory, energy is associated with time (t) while the momentum is associated with the space coordinates (x in one dimension). However, energy enters the quantum wave equation linearly (as $E \sim t$) and momentum enters as the square (as $p^2 \sim x^2$), which means that the equation is not symmetrical in time and space. To Schrödinger's despair, when he modified the equation according to the space–time symmetry requirement, it was still unable to reproduce the correct fine structure spectrum. There was something wrong, but he could not figure out what it was.

Nonetheless, in the summer of 1926 Schrödinger published the relativistic version of his wave equation and so did half a dozen other physicists. Pauli called it "the equation with the many fathers." Because two of the "fathers" were Oskar Klein and Walter Gordon, a Swedish and German physicist respectively, it became known as the Klein-Gordon equation. It was a nice but apparently useless formula. The problem with relativity was not exclusive to wave mechanics for it also appeared in matrix mechanics and Dirac's q-number algebra. After all, the three formulations were just different versions of the same theory, quantum mechanics.

There was another and possibly related problem. To characterize the behavior of an electron, it must be ascribed a "spin" quantum number that can attain only two values, $+\frac{1}{2}$ or $-\frac{1}{2}$. In the classical picture, it corresponds to a spherical charge that rotates around its axis in either of the two directions. Spin was discovered in the summer of 1925 and initially seemed foreign to the new quantum mechanics. It could be grafted upon the quantum equations but not derived from them. Physicists vaguely realized that spin and relativity were somewhat connected, but nobody could tell in what way or how they fit into the formalism of quantum mechanics. Attempts to make them fit were *ad hoc* and did not appeal to Dirac at all. He was slowly getting interested in the spin puzzle, and in December of 1926, when he stayed with Heisenberg in Copenhagen, the two physicists made a bet of when spin would be properly explained. Dirac thought three months, Heisenberg, at least, three years. They were both wrong, but Heisenberg more than Dirac. (The process took one year).

A little more than three months after the bet, Pauli came up with a quantum-mechanical theory of spin, if not a proper explanation. His idea was to extend Schrödinger's wave function ψ from one to two components. An electron would then be characterized by (ψ_1, ψ_2) where the two functions represented the electron's two spin states by means of new variables. The variables were 2 × 2 "Pauli matrices" with two rows and two columns. Pauli's theory made sense of the spin within the framework of ordinary quantum mechanics, but since it was not relativistic, Dirac considered it to be merely a provisional solution. The easy way would be to integrate spin and the Klein-Gordon equation, but this turned out not to be possible. It was Dirac who solved the problem and perhaps won the bet with Heisenberg. However, the solution came in a roundabout way. "I was not interested in bringing the spin of the electron into the wave equation," he recalled. "It was a great surprise to me when I later discovered that the simplest possible case did involve the spin." Dirac's discovery was an example of what is called *serendipity*, the almost accidental discovery of something the scientist is not looking for.

Having no faith in the Klein-Gordon equation, at the end of 1927 Dirac decided to find a better solution for a wave equation in accordance with the theory of relativity. Based on the relativity requirement and the general structure of quantum mechanics, he was convinced that the equation he looked for must be linear not only in energy, as in the ordinary Schrödinger equation, but also in momentum. This conviction brought him face to face with a purely mathematical problem, namely how to write the square root of a sum of four squares as a linear combination. Take the square root of $(a^2 + b^2 + c^2 + d^2)$ and try to write it as $n_1a + n_2b + n_3c + n_4d$, where the n's are some coefficients. That's not an easy problem, but Dirac needed to solve it. Guided by Pauli's spin matrices and his own mathematical intuition, he realized that the trick could be done if the n-coefficients were 4 × 4 matrices, that is, quantities with four rows and columns comprising 16 numbers. With these "Dirac matrices," he could straightforwardly write down the new wave equation for a free electron. As a consequence of the 4 × 4 matrices, the wave function had not only two components, as in Pauli's theory, but four: $\psi = (\psi_1, \psi_2, \psi_3, \psi_4)$.

The crucial step in Dirac's derivation was the reduction of a physical problem to a mathematical one. The method was characteristic of his style of physics. "A great deal of my work is just playing with equations and seeing what they give," Dirac said in a 1963 interview. "I think it's a peculiarity of myself that I like to play about with equations, just looking for beautiful relations which maybe can't have any physical meaning at all. Sometimes they do." In this case, they did.

And what about the spin? Dirac had originally ignored the problem by considering, for reasons of simplicity, an electron without spin, knowing that such a particle did not exist. But when he extended his wave equation of the free electron to one where the electron interacted with an electromagnetic field, he discovered that the correct spin appeared, almost mysteriously. Without introducing the spin in advance, Dirac was able to deduce the electron's spin from the first principles upon which his equation was built. In a certain if somewhat unhistorical sense, had spin not been discovered experimentally, it would have turned up deductively in Dirac's theory. This was a great and unexpected triumph. It was less unexpected but still very satisfactory that the equation could account in detail for the fine structure of the hydrogen spectrum.

Dirac submitted his paper on the new electron theory on the first day of 1928, and it appeared in print a month later. It came as a bombshell to the physics community. Dirac had worked alone, almost secretly, not for reasons of priority but because it was his habit. His senior colleague Charles Darwin, a professor at the University of Edinburgh and a grandson of the "real Darwin," was one of the few who knew in advance what was going on. In a letter to Bohr of December 26, 1927, he wrote: "I was at Cambridge a few days ago and saw Dirac. He has now got a completely new system of equations for the electron, which does the spin right in all cases and seems to be 'the thing.' His equations are first order, not second, differential equations!" Dirac's equation was indeed the thing. It was received with equal measures of surprise and enthusiasm—even by the physicists who had come close to solving the problem themselves. Among them was Jordan, who, in this case, lost to Dirac. A physicist who at the time worked in Göttingen recalled: "The general feeling was that Dirac had had more than he deserved! Doing physics in that way was not done! … [The Dirac equation] was immediately seen as *the* solution. It was regarded really as an absolute wonder."

The new relativistic theory of the electron had a revolutionary effect on quantum physics, both pure and applied. It was as if it had a life of its own, full of surprises and subtleties undreamed of even by Dirac when he worked it out. For example, the 4 × 4 Dirac matrices attracted much interest among the pure mathematicians who eagerly studied the properties of the matrices and other mathematical objects related to them. This branch of mathematical physics eventually developed into a minor industry and is still an active field of research. Right after Dirac's theory appeared, it seemed that although it had great explanatory power, there was no particular predictive power. It explained the electron's spin and hydrogen's fine structure most beautifully, but no predictions of novel phenomena followed from it. This situation soon changed. Within a few years, Dirac's equation and the electron theory based on it proved successful over a wide range of physical areas, including high-energy scattering processes and the mysterious cosmic rays. Most dramatically, it led to the successful prediction of a new class of elementary particles, which Dirac called antiparticles.

The revolutionary concept of antimatter or antiparticles had its roots in conceptual problems of the Dirac equation noted at an early date. In the four-component wave function (ψ_1, ψ_2, ψ_3, ψ_4) two of the components, say ψ_1 and ψ_2, refer to the two spin states of an ordinary electron, just as in Pauli's theory. What do ψ_3 and ψ_4 refer to? They enter because Dirac's theory is a quantum translation of the energy-momentum relation in relativity theory, which involves the *squares* of energy and momentum. But Dirac's equation, following the basic rules of quantum mechanics, was linear in energy. It involved E and not E^2. Now, when you take the square root of mc^2 you don't get just the energy E but also the negative quantity − E. After all, $(- E)^2 = E^2$. Formally ψ_3 and ψ_4 refer to the two spin states of a negatively charged electron with *negative energy*. We can avoid negative-energy electrons, but in that case, the two wave functions need to be interpreted as belonging to electrons of positive charge. As Dirac pointed out in 1930, "an electron with negative energy moves in an external field as though it carries a positive charge."

Both interpretations invited trouble. Take the hypothetical negative-energy (and negative-charge) electrons. Since energy is equivalent to mass by $E = mc^2$, the mass of a negative-energy electron at rest will also be negative. It can easily be shown that the energy of such a particle, when set in motion, will decrease the faster it moves; moreover, when a force is impressed on the particle, it will accelerate in the opposite direction of the force. Absurd! The Russian physicist George Gamow had first met Dirac in 1927, and the two established a lasting friendship. Gamow called the negative-energy electrons formally occurring in Dirac's theory "donkey electrons"—the harder they were pushed, the slower they would move. From the standpoint of physics, by 1930 the positive-electron interpretation was no better, for the charge of electrons was known to be negative. Earlier speculations about positive electrons had turned out to be just that—speculations. The only known positive particle—or "positive electron"—was the proton, which is nearly 2,000 times heavier than an electron. According to the paradigm governing physics at the time, there were no other massive elementary particles than the electron and the proton (the photon has no mass). The dilemma was this: either one had to postulate electrons with negative energy that behaved absurdly or the existence of a particle for which there was not the slightest empirical evidence. As a third possibility, one might have discarded Dirac's theory *in toto*, but this was an option no one seriously considered. There was no way back.

The intertwined problems of the energy and charge of Dirac's electron were much debated in the physics community. Heisenberg, Jordan, and others were deeply worried about what they called the "± difficulty." For example, in 1928 Jordan referred to "the murky problem of the asymmetry of the forms of electricity, that is, the inequality of mass for positive and negative electrons." In relation to this problem, he judged that Dirac's "theory is entangled in temporarily insoluble difficulties." Heisenberg concurred: "The saddest chapter of modern physics is and remains the Dirac theory." Dirac was worried too, but in the late autumn of 1929, he thought to have found an answer to the ± difficulty. His hypothesis was as original as it was audacious—vintage Dirac. He first reported it in letters to Bohr, through which it became known to other physicists, and publicly announced his "Theory of Electrons and Protons" in a paper written in early 1930.

Dirac realized that particles with negative energy could have no reality in nature, and he consequently focused on the ± difficulty in the sense of the hypothetical positive electrons. This is not to say that he just ignored the negative energy problem, but he made the negative-energy electrons invisible, so to speak. Dirac boldly assumed a world of negative-energy states uniformly occupied by an infinite number of electrons with energies extending from $- mc^2$ to minus infinity. If this distribution of negative-energy electrons in the "Dirac sea" were exactly uniform, they would be unobservable, merely serving to define a state of normal electrification. Dirac identified it with the vacuum. As he wrote to Bohr, "On my new theory the state of negative energy has a physical meaning, but the electron cannot jump down into it because it is already occupied." This was a result of Pauli's fundamental exclusion principle, according to which two electrons cannot occupy the same quantum state. Pauli suggested the principle in 1925 to explain the periodic system of the chemical elements, and in 1945, he was belatedly awarded the Nobel Prize for his discovery.

Had Dirac just postulated his world to be filled up with negative-energy electrons and governed by the Pauli principle, it would have been nothing but a metaphysical idea: it would have had no measurable consequences. But he further assumed that a few of the negative-energy states might be unoccupied, and in this case, it would be possible for a real, positive-energy electron to "jump" into one of the unoccupied states, and fill it. The vacant states or "holes" would appear as real physical entities: "Only the small departures from exact uniformity, brought about by some of the negative-energy states being unoccupied, can we hope to observe," he noted. "These holes will be things of positive energy and will therefore be in this respect like ordinary particles."

The idea of holes enabled Dirac to account for the negative-energy solutions that formally turned up in his theory without having to introduce observable negative-energy particles. But what were these holes or things? Dirac thought at first that the holes were protons—or, for that matter, that electrons were holes in a negative-energy proton sea. The two particles were basically the same, the proton being an electron in disguise and the electron a proton in disguise. "We are," he wrote in 1930, "led to the assumption that the holes in the distribution of negative-energy electrons are the protons."

By identifying the proton with a vacant negative-energy state, he had effectively reduced all elementary particles known at the time to just one fundamental entity, the electron. This was a unifying idea that appealed greatly to Dirac, as he made clear in an address he gave in September of 1930. It has always been "the dream of philosophers" to explain all matter in terms of just one entity, Dirac said, boldly suggesting that it was no longer just a dream. "There are ... reasons for believing that the electron and proton are really not independent, but are just two manifestations of one elementary kind of particle." He ended *Principles of Quantum Mechanics*, published a few months earlier, with the same dramatic message.

Dirac was almost alone in defending the electron-proton hypothesis, which most of his colleagues in physics considered wildly speculative and unreasonable. While some criticized it on technical grounds, others simply wrote it off as nonsense. The grand and beautiful hypothesis was not nonsense, but it was wrong: it faced two serious empirical problems, which neither Dirac nor other physicists were able to escape.

According to the hypothesis, one would expect that an ordinary electron would occasionally make a quantum transition to fill a hole. In that case, it would annihilate together with the hole, or proton, and the mass of the two particles would transform into radiation energy in accordance with Einstein's $E = mc^2$ formula. Annihilation processes of this kind, $e^- + p^+ \rightarrow$ radiation, had been considered by several astronomers as a possible source of stellar energy, but they had never been observed in either nature or the laboratory. Dirac was well aware that the process was without experimental evidence and yet he optimistically stated that "There seems to be no reason why such processes should not actually occur somewhere in the world." The lack of evidence for electron–proton annihilation indicated that the frequency of such processes was exceedingly small and perhaps zero. Unfortunately, when physicists calculated the probability of proton–electron annihilation on the basis of Dirac's theory, they came up with large and not small numbers. According to Oppenheimer, if Dirac were right, then all matter would long ago have disappeared and left a universe filled entirely by radiation.

The other problem was more obvious, namely that the proton is much heavier than the electron. Heisenberg had pointed out as early as December of 1929 that in Dirac's theory the two particles—the electron and the hole/proton—must have the same mass; his objection was confirmed by calculations made by other physicists. Dirac tried for a while to explain the embarrassing mass difference, but in the end, he was forced to conclude that his unitary hypothesis was wrong. He did it with regret, especially because he found the hypothesis very attractive.

The capitulation did not mean that Dirac abandoned his imagery of an infinitely deep sea filled (or almost filled) with negative-energy electrons. He just revised it, offering a new candidate for the holes. He did this in a remarkable paper of June 1931. The groundbreaking idea of antiparticles was only dealt with casually, for the main subject of the paper was the possible existence of magnetic monopoles. After admitting that the earlier electron–proton idea was no longer tenable, Dirac wrote: "A hole, if there were one, would be a new kind of particle, unknown to experimental physics, having the same mass and opposite charge to an electron. We may call such a particle an anti-electron." He further suggested that antielectrons were probably very rare in nature and might never be found, but "if they could be produced experimentally in high vacuum they would be quite stable and amenable to observation." There is no doubt that Dirac considered the antielectron to be a real particle, as he made clear in a talk he gave at Princeton in the fall of 1931, emphasizing that anti-electrons "are not to be considered as a mathematical fiction." As a means of possible detection, he introduced the notion of what has become known as pair production, the formation of a particle-antiparticle pair out of radiation energy.

Within the space of one page, Dirac predicted two new elementary particles in addition to the two already known empirically. The proton was no longer the antiparticle of the electron and therefore supposedly had its own mirror particle: "Presumably the protons will have their own negative-energy states, all of which normally are occupied, an unoccupied one appearing as an anti-proton." That was all, but in some of his later papers Dirac elaborated on the idea of matter made up of antiparticles, by which he meant antielectrons and antiprotons. Although the neutron was discovered in 1932, he never mentioned the antineutron (which has the same zero charge as the neutron, but differs from it in other respects). Dirac, the paragon of a rational physicist, was not a stranger to speculation, as illustrated in his 1933 Nobel lecture. On this occasion, he suggested that it might be a coincidence that our solar system consists almost solely of ordinary protons and electrons. "It is quite probable," he said, "that for some of the stars it is the other way about, these stars being built up mainly of positrons and negative protons. In fact, there may be half the stars of each kind. The two kinds of stars would both show the same spectra, and there would be no way of distinguishing them by present astronomical methods." Dirac stopped short of speculating about anti-humans.

Many physicists considered Dirac's prediction of a positive electron to be as poorly justified as his earlier proton hypothesis. Both ideas were based on the theory of holes, which was widely regarded with skepticism or as merely a provisional picture. Bohr and Pauli sided against the hole theory and its idea of antiparticles as vacancies in a sea of negative energy states. Their dislike persisted even after the positive electron was discovered. After all, even though Dirac had predicted a positive electron from the hole theory, it did not mean that the discovery of the particle proved the theory right. There were other ways through which the new particle could be better justified.

From the 1933 Copenhagen conference at Niels Bohr's Institute. Dirac is seated in the first row between Bohr and Heisenberg. Credit: Niels Bohr Archive, Copenhagen.

In April of 1932, Bohr's institute in Copenhagen celebrated its 10th anniversary in the presence of a large number of quantum physicists, including Pauli, Dirac, Ehrenfest, Gamow, Klein, Darwin and Bohr himself. The participants staged a parody of Goethe's *Faust*, adapted to the situation in theoretical physics as it was at that time. Part of the memorable play dealt with Dirac's hole theory and the criticism of it. Dirac's part was as follows:

> That donkey-electrons should wander
> Quite aimless through space, is a slander,
> That only with articles
> On hole-like particles
> Could be said to have found a defender.

To which Bohr replied:

> But the point of the fact is remaining

That we cannot refrain from complaining,
That such a caprice
Will reveal the malice
Of devouring the world it's sustaining.

Physics textbooks often portray the actual discovery of the positive electron as a classical example of the fruitful interplay between theory and experiment. A theory predicts a novel object or phenomenon in nature, which is subsequently investigated experimentally and actually found to exist. As theory guides the discovery, so the discovery confirms the theory. The authentic discovery history of the positive electron is more complex and less morally suited for textbooks. The brief version is that in 1932, Carl Anderson, a California experimental physicist, found tracks in cloud chambers in the upper atmosphere that he interpreted as positive particles in the cosmic rays. He did not originally suggest they were positive electrons, which he only postulated in a paper the following year, where he also proposed the convenient name "positron" for the new particle (and the logically reasonable but less successful "negatron" for the ordinary electron).

Anderson discovered the positron in 1933 but not Dirac's antielectron. Many years later, Anderson remarked: "Despite the fact that Dirac's relativistic theory of the electron was an adequate theory of the positron, and despite the fact that the existence of this theory was well known to nearly all physicists, it played no part whatsoever in the discovery of the positron." It was only after further cosmic rays experiments carried out at about the same time by the London physicist Patrick Blackett and his Italian collaborator Giuseppe Occhialini that it was realized that Anderson's positron was Dirac's antielectron. Not only was Blackett aware of Dirac's theory, but while working in Cambridge, he also discussed his experiments and their theoretical significance with Dirac. In their 1933 paper, Blackett and Occhialini referred explicitly to the antielectron, suggesting that the positive electron supported Dirac's theory. Anderson and Blackett would both be awarded a Nobel Prize for their work on cosmic rays particles, the first in 1936 and the latter in 1948.

After 1933, the fundamental idea of antiparticles was generally accepted, especially after it was shown that antiparticles could be accounted for without relying on Dirac's somewhat fanciful picture of a sea of unobservable negative-energy particles. With or without this picture, the prediction of antiparticles was considered a marvel. Heisenberg once called it "perhaps the biggest jump of all big jumps in physics of our century." This was an apt description, for a jump it was. With the benefit of hindsight, Dirac later said that the idea of antimatter "really follows directly from Einstein's special theory of relativity when it is combined with the quantum mechanics of Heisenberg." But he downplayed his own genius and the creative element in the discovery of antimatter. If it had been as simple as he said, antimatter would have been discovered by one of the dozen physicists who sought a relativistic version of quantum mechanics before Dirac, perhaps by Schrödinger, Klein, or Pauli. But it wasn't. To an almost unparalleled extent in the history of science, antimatter was due to the creative mind of just one scientist.

For a long time, antiparticles meant positrons, whereas the antiproton (or negative proton) was rarely discussed. But with the entrance of still more powerful accelerators into the elementary particle physics, the antiproton also turned out to be real. It was first detected in high-energy experiments in 1955, and today antiprotons are produced routinely and in large numbers. The antineutron followed in 1956. As Dirac had speculated just over two decades earlier, matter consisting purely of antiparticles might actually exist somewhere in the universe. Whether or not cosmic antimatter exists, since 1996 the simplest form of antimatter has been produced in the laboratory. The short-lived anti-hydrogen atom is made up of a positron revolving round an antiproton. Anti-helium nuclei (but not atoms) have also been detected.

By 1950, it was recognized that the particle-antiparticle symmetry is a fundamental law of nature. We call the positron the antiparticle of the electron, but we might just as well have called the electron the antiparticle of the positron. Matter has no priority over antimatter, except that our universe has much more matter than antimatter. The perfect symmetry between the two kinds of matter remained a mystery for a long time. Could Dirac's speculation of 1933 be more than just a wild idea? More than 30 years later, there had been attempts to establish a "plasma cosmology" on the assumption that the universe originally consisted of equal amounts of matter and antimatter, the Big Bang being a gigantic explosion of matter annihilating with antimatter. Plasma cosmology, still cultivated by a few physicists, attracted only limited scientific interest and Dirac never mentioned the hypothesis.

With the recognition of the hot Big Bang model in the 1960s, the challenge no longer consisted of explaining why there was so little antimatter, but in elucidating why there was some at all. If antimatter were as abundant as matter in the very early and dense universe, almost all antiparticles would have annihilated with particles, leaving a universe consisting of photons and only insignificant traces of matter. Obviously, this "annihilation catastrophe" did not occur—if it had, we would not exist. How could an initially symmetrical universe have evolved into the world like the one we know? Only at the time of Dirac's death in 1984 did physicists believe to have found an answer. It was vaguely related to another of Dirac's ideas, namely that the laws of physics are not static but have evolved over time. The kind of "grand unified" law that governed the very early universe allowed a slight preponderance of matter over antimatter, and thereby, prevented the annihilation catastrophe. This explanation essentially solved the mystery.

The antielectron was originally a pretty wild idea based on an abstract theory of quantum mechanics, and the positron was an elusive and exotic particle of interest only to pure physics. Today, many hospitals are equipped with PET scanners, an acronym for positron-electron tomography. The patient is injected with a radioactive isotope, which emits positrons, and the positrons annihilate with the electrons in the tissue. As a result of the annihilation, a pair of well-defined photons is emitted. By registering the photonic signals, a computer image of some inner part of the patient is produced. The first versions of PET scanning technology were developed when Dirac was still alive. Had he known about the technology (which he probably did not), he might have been pleased to see how his old prediction had morphed into a useful medical imaging instrument. But it is more likely that he wouldn't have cared—medical imaging by means of positrons is not fundamental physics.

4

Monopoleon

The antielectron as a hypothetical elementary particle first appeared in Dirac's paper in 1931, which also contained the first proposal of the antiproton. Yet the paper—Gamow once called it the last important paper in theoretical physics—was about something else. It introduced yet another hypothetical particle, no less strange than the antielectron. The particle is called a magnetic monopole and its fate in the history of modern physics is entirely different from that of the antielectron. To this day, the magnetic monopole—or just the monopole—remains merely an idea.

Consider a bar magnet consisting of a north pole at one end and a south pole at the other. If you cut it into two parts, you will not end up with two isolated poles but with just two smaller magnets, or "dipoles," each with a north and a south pole. You may go on forever without isolating a magnetic pole. It is an empirical fact that while positive and negative electrical charges exist in nature, there are no corresponding magnetic charges or poles. The absence of magnetic monopoles is encoded in the fundamental Maxwell equations, which otherwise exhibit a nice symmetry between electricity and magnetism.

The Maxwell equations forbid monopoles, but only because the lack of monopoles in nature is built into the equations. One can easily modify the equations to accommodate monopoles, should such a particle be found.

In the absence of empirical evidence, the possible existence of monopoles attracted little attention in classical physics. In a few cases, physicists believed to have discovered phenomena that revealed the existence of the magnetic poles, but it quickly turned out that the claims were unfounded. When quantum mechanics arrived, it became even more difficult to believe in these hypothetical entities. The reason is that the quantum theory of the electromagnetic field relies on quantities that effectively rule out monopoles. In a nutshell, magnetic monopoles are inconsistent with quantum electrodynamics. Given this situation, it is understandable that monopoles were simply not an issue in the new physics—until 1931.

Why would Dirac reconsider something, which all quantum physicists knew did not and could not exist? The answer is that he did not, but he came to the idea in the same roundabout way that characterized some of his other discoveries. The monopole was yet another example of serendipity, as Dirac later explained: "It often happens in scientific research that when one is looking for one thing, one is led to discover something that one wasn't expecting. This is what happened to me with the monopole concept. I was not searching for anything like monopoles at the time." The "thing" he was looking for in 1931 was, as he stated at the beginning of the paper, "the reason for the existence of a smallest electric charge."

Free electrical charges always appear as multiples of the smallest charge, called the elementary charge and denoted e. Whatever charge Q is, it always can be written as $Q = ne$, where n is a whole number. For example, for an electron $n = -1$ and for a calcium ion $n = +2$. The quantization of charge had been experimentally established in the 1910s and was doubted by no one. But *why* is charge quantized and *why* is the smallest charge e rather than something else? These were the questions that Dirac ambitiously addressed. If he could derive e from a fundamental theory, he would also have derived the strength of the electromagnetic force as given by the so-called fine-structure constant usually assigned the symbol α. This constant, as famous as it is enigmatic, is also the quantity determining the details of the hydrogen spectrum, as Dirac had explained it in his electron theory of 1928. It is a dimensionless number with the approximate value 1/137 or about 0.0073. Again, why this value? Dirac wanted to find out and physicists today still want to know. The value of α is known with great precision, but, as Richard Feynman put it, "It's one of the *greatest* damn mysteries of physics: a *magic number* that comes to us with no understanding by man."

Dirac was forced to admit that he could not solve the problem he had initially addressed. His efforts were not wasted, though, for while pondering the problem he reached the surprising conclusion that magnetic monopoles were *not* ruled out by either electrodynamics or quantum mechanics.

In a lengthy introduction to his 1931 paper, Dirac reflected on the relationship between physics and mathematics, a subject he would return to on later occasions. In a general sense, he suggested that the inductive method starting with experimental data was unlikely to lead to progress in modern theoretical physics. Relativity theory relied on abstract mathematical ideas such as non-Euclidean geometry and quantum mechanics on no less abstract mathematics, like non-commuting algebra. Dirac advocated a deductive method based on mathematics, namely, "to employ all the resources of pure mathematics in attempts to perfect and generalise the mathematical formalism that forms the existing basis of theoretical physics, and *after* each success in this direction, to try to interpret the new mathematical features in terms of physical entities." This was the method underlying Dirac's own theory of holes—"a small step according to this general scheme of advance"—and now he used the same method to reconsider the magnetic monopole problem.

Dirac's approach was complex, relying on a careful analysis of the mathematical structure of the wave function ψ appearing in quantum mechanics. He essentially demonstrated that without changing the basic structure it was possible to "perfect and generalise" the wave function in such a way that monopoles were possible objects, that is, consistent with quantum mechanics. A few pages of dense calculations were enough to prove that quantum mechanics under certain conditions could be brought to accommodate monopoles. The strength G of the magnetic poles turned out to be quantized in the same sense as the strength Q of electrical charges. As there exists a smallest electrical charge e, so there must exist a smallest magnetic charge g, the two being inversely proportional (eg = constant). To Dirac's dismay, he was unable to calculate either e or g separately from pure theory, which he found to be "rather disappointing."

Nevertheless, Dirac demonstrated that the hitherto inexplicable quantization of electricity would be explained *if* monopoles existed. From the e–g relationship he had derived between electricity and magnetism, it followed that a north pole and a south pole would form a strongly bound system, kept together much more strongly than a positive and negative elementary charge. It would, therefore, take a very large energy to break up an elementary dipole made up of monopoles. More precisely, two elementary poles of opposite sign will attract one another with a force nearly 5,000 times greater than that between two elementary charges at the same distance. This consequence of his theory was featured a year later in the *Faust* parody at Bohr's Copenhagen Institute:

Two monopoles worshiped each other,

And all of their sentiments clicked.
Still, neither could get to his brother,
Dirac was so fearfully strict!

It is one thing to prove theoretically that an object is allowed according to fundamental physics, but quite another to claim that the object actually exists in either nature or laboratory. Dirac believed that his antielectrons and monopoles really existed. Referring to the consistency with quantum mechanics, he concluded, "Under these circumstances one would be surprised if Nature had not made use of it." But if magnetic monopoles existed out there, why had they not been observed? One reason, Dirac suggested, might have been the strong coupling between two opposite poles.

"Lonely magnetic poles may change ideas of the universe," *Science News Letter* reported on April 16, 1932, adding that scientists could use the new particles in "postulating how the universe is put together." However, no revolution in our world picture occurred, and interest in Dirac's theory soon waned. Although well known to the physics community, Dirac's theory attracted relatively little attention and even less acceptance. Pauli found the theory to be satisfactory from a logical and mathematical point of view, yet he was skeptical about the actual existence of monopoles. In a 1949 letter, he sarcastically referred to Dirac as "Monopoleon."

The main reason for the lukewarm response was that the monopole was not very useful. It was allowed according to theory, but not required to solve any of the problems with which the physicists struggled at the time. In short, it appeared to be superfluous. And then, of course, it was unsupported by experimental evidence. All in all, there were good reasons why the monopole did not cause excitement among the physicists. When the Nobel Committee evaluated Dirac as a candidate, it expressed a view probably shared by many physicists. The 1931 monopole paper, the Committee opined, was "strongly speculative but of pretty much interest to those who are not afraid of speculation."

The only physicist of repute who was sympathetic to and seriously interested in Dirac's theory was his colleague and sometime rival Pascual Jordan, who greatly admired Dirac's approach to physics. In a 1938 paper, he carefully investigated the new theory, suggesting that magnetic poles might be more than just mathematical constructs. In 1931, the accepted number of elementary particles was just two

Sketches of Dirac by an unknown artist from "Blegdamsvejens Faust," a parody staged by physicists at Bohr's institute in April 1932. In the upper right, Dirac keeps two oppositely charged monopoles apart, while the figure below refers to Dirac's hole theory. An electron—in the round shape of the physicist Charles G. Darwin—dives into the Dirac sea. Credit: Niels Bohr Archive, Copenhagen.

(electron and proton), but since then the number had increased considerably. Not only had the neutron and the positron been discovered, the neutrino and the muon (then called a "mesotron") had also won acceptance, and physicists expected to find even more particles. In this situation, Jordan pointed out, "one would now rather be inclined to regard the Dirac pole as a possibility worthy of serious investigation."

One might expect that Dirac himself promoted the magnetic monopole, his brainchild, but this was not the case at all. He apparently lost interest in his theory, to which he only returned 17 years later. In a 1948 paper, Dirac revised and greatly improved the theoretical foundation of monopole physics, now basing it closely on the more advanced framework of quantum electrodynamics. The paper was mathematically impressive and theoretically innovative, the kind that was hardly understandable to the average physicist. But it did not provide much new physical insight. Nor did it succeed in explaining the quantization of electricity and magnetism from first principles, which had been Dirac's original motivation. He did, however, calculate how a monopole would interact with matter—for example, when it passed a photographic plate. Ordinary charged particles leave an ionization track that broadens as the particles slow down, but, Dirac argued, a monopole would behave quite differently. If caught in a plate, its track would remain roughly constant. In this way, Dirac indicated a method of potential use for future monopole hunters.

At the time of Dirac's 1948 paper, there had been only a few searches for magnetic poles, none of which was even remotely successful. It took another two decades until experimentalists got seriously interested and devised methods to catch the elusive particle, if it existed at all. With improvements in high-energy technology and the proliferation of new elementary particles, the magnetic monopole was no longer considered to be beyond experimental discovery. It was an exotic particle, but scarcely more exotic than other hypothetical particles in the zoo of high-energy physics. The monopole was now raised to the status of a "well-known missing particle," a respectable object to hunt by the fast-growing community of high-energy experimentalists.

In 1975, a team of American physicists announced that they had discovered in balloon-born experiments a cosmic-rays particle with the properties that Dirac had predicted. The announcement attracted much media interest, including a suggestion in the *New York Times* that the discovery would most likely lead to "new medical therapies in the fight against diseases such as cancer, and new sources of energy." Alas, the much-publicized claim turned out to be unfounded and after some controversy, it was retracted.

History repeated itself seven years later when Blas Cabrera, an experienced physicist at Stanford University, detected a signal with the telltale characteristics of a Dirac monopole. It was measured on February 14, 1982, and is therefore known in physicists' lore as the

Valentine day event. A year later, Cabrera received a Valentine card from a group of Harvard physicists headed by Sheldon Glashow, a particle theorist and Nobel laureate of 1979. It said:

> Roses are red, violets are blue.
> The time has come for monopole two.

No monopole number two ever passed through Cabrera's or someone else's detector. A single event was not enough to change the status of the monopole from being a well-known missing particle to one really existing.

It is ironic that monopole physics only began to flourish after the death of its originator. During the last couple of decades, hundreds of papers have been written on the subject, some of them theoretical and others experimental. Many still refer to Dirac's old papers, which until the present have received a total of nearly 5,000 citations in scientific journals. However, the monopoles, which have attracted most interest in modern physics, are not quite the same as Dirac's.

In the mid-1970s, it was shown that early versions of the so-called grand unified theory predicted a new kind of monopole that complied with Dirac's quantization rule eg = constant. But the GUMs (Grand Unified Monopoles) are exceedingly massive and rather than being point-like in the way that the Dirac monopoles were, they are endowed with a complex inner structure. Much of the present interest in GUMs and monopoles, in general, is cosmologically motivated. The reason is that according to some models, these magnetic particles were produced in copious amounts at the birth of the universe. Based on grand unified theory, it was estimated that the number of primordial monopoles was enormous even if annihilation with anti-monopoles was taken into account (strangely, Dirac never mentioned the anti-monopole). But then, what happened to all these particles? Why has a monopole never been seen?

While trying to answer this question in 1979, Alan Guth, a 31-year-old particle physicist at Cornell University came up with the idea of the inflating universe. This hypothesis suggested that in an exceedingly brief span of time after the Big Bang, the universe expanded at a phenomenal rate. According to Guth, the monopoles did not disappear, but because of the extreme dilution following the inflation they became so rare that it is unlikely that we should ever be able to meet one. The inflation theory, in one of its many versions, is today widely accepted, even if still considered controversial by some cosmologists.

So, does the particle first proposed by Dirac more than 80 years ago exist or not? We don't know. Dirac himself eventually lost faith in the particle he had so boldly invented. His last comment on the subject was in a letter from 1981: "I am inclined now to believe that monopoles do not exist."

5

On the Road

"**H**e was the prototype of the superior mathematical mind; but while in others this had coexisted with a multitude of interests, in Dirac's case everything went into the performance of his great historical mission, the establishment of the new science, quantum mechanics, to which he probably contributed as much as any other man." This was how the German physicist Walter Elsasser characterized Dirac. Elsasser, who was a student of Born and later in life, would turn to a distinguished career in the earth sciences, had first met Dirac in Göttingen in 1927, and later, on several other occasions. Recall that in 1927, Raymond Birge had observed that "Dirac thinks of absolutely nothing but physics." While it is true that Dirac's life was very much focused on physics, these two statements exaggerate his singular mindset. Dirac did have other interests. One of them was chess, a game he played very well and as often as he could, both in Cambridge and abroad. He served for many years as president of the chess club of St. John's College.

More important than his interest in chess was Dirac's insatiable appetite for travel. At a time when the concept of global tourism was not yet developed, Dirac traveled all over the world. Many of his trips were connected with conferences and lectures while others were just vacations. His idea of a holiday, however, was not relaxing at a resort hotel near a sunny beach. More typically, it involved long and strenuous hikes on difficult terrains.

Dirac's idea of a pleasant vacation may be illustrated by the first of his many visits to the Soviet Union. While staying in Göttingen in 1928, he was invited to an international physics conference that took part in Moscow and continued aboard a steamboat along the Volga River. After the conference had ended, Dirac traveled alone through the Caucasus to the Black Sea coast, using the occasion to climb a mountain to the altitude of about 3,000 meters (10,000 feet). Then, as

Dirac in Göttingen, 1928. Credit: Niels Bohr Archive, Copenhagen.

he reported to Tamm upon his return to Cambridge: "I spent three days in Tiflis [Tbilisi, the present capital of Georgia], mostly resting and making up for lost sleep, and then went to Batoum [Batumi, a seaside city in Georgia] to try to get a boat for Constantinople." After a couple of days and much trouble, he succeeded in getting a Turkish visa. "From Constantinople I took a ship to Marseilles, visiting Athens and Naples on the way, and then I came home across France and ended a most pleasant holiday." During another visit to the Soviet Union eight years later, Dirac, Tamm, and a group of other Russians climbed the 5,640-meter (18,510-feet) Mount Elbrus in the Caucasus Mountains. The leader of the expedition recalled how he tried in vain to get Dirac to accept the "USSR Alpine Climber" badge for having reached the top of Europe's highest mountain.

Dirac was also a great walker who had the stamina and physical energy that surprised those who knew him only from conferences and dinner parties. During the Christmas of 1935, he went to visit Margit Wigner in Austria, whom he would marry two years later. She recalled: "He used to go off for long walks; he knew no fatigue, meals were unimportant to him, but not to me. ... I often accompanied Paul, but usually regretted it. His enduring capacity would have been too much for most mortals." Lack of personal comfort never bothered Dirac, who for a long time lived an almost ascetic life. He never touched alcoholic drinks and never smoked. "Dirac is rather like one's idea of Gandhi," wrote a Cambridge physicist in a letter in 1931. "He is quite indifferent to cold, discomfort, food etc. We had him to ... a nice little supper here, but I am sure he would not have minded if we had only given him porridge."

In the spring of 1929, Dirac paid his first visit to the United States to take up a position as a visiting professor at the University of Wisconsin in Madison. In a humorous interview in the local *Wisconsin State Journal,* the strange creature from Europe was introduced as "a mathematical physicist, or something, they call him—who is pushing Sir Isaac Newton, Einstein and all the others off the front page." So the interviewer paid a visit to the new professor and reported: "His name is Dirac and he is an Englishman. He has been given lectures for the intelligentsia of the math and physics department—and a few other guys who got in by mistake. ... I knock at the door of Dr. Dirac's office in Sterling Hall and a pleasant voice says 'Come in.' And I want to say here and now that this sentence 'come in' was about the longest one emitted by the doctor during our interview. He sure is for efficiency in conversation. ... The thing that hit me in the eye about him was that he did not seem to be at all busy. ... He seems to have all the time there is in the world and his heaviest work is looking out of the window. If he is a typical Englishman it's me for England on my next vacation!"

Having completed his lectures in Wisconsin, Dirac traveled extensively through the United States, visiting, among other places, Chicago, Los Angeles, the Grand Canyon, and the Yosemite National Park. The summer of 1929 found him in Berkeley, where he gave lectures on quantum mechanics. Heisenberg was also lecturing in Berkeley at the time, and since they had both been invited to Japan, the two quantum pioneers decided to go together and return to Europe westward. Dirac and Heisenberg left San Francisco on a steamer that brought them to Hawaii and from there on to Japan. After having completed their lectures in Tokyo the two young physicists separated. While Heisenberg returned to Europe by boat, Dirac insisted on taking the harder way to Siberia. He had originally planned to go through Manchuria, but troubles at the Chinese–Soviet border prevented it. "I shall leave Vladivostok in the early morning," he wrote from Kyoto to Tamm. "I cannot remember the exact time of my arrival in Moscow and have left my time-table in Tokyo, but as there is now only one train a week from Vladivostok I expect you will be able to find it out without difficulty." From the Russian capital, Dirac went to Leningrad by train and from there to Berlin by airplane—probably his first experience in the air. Train and ship finally brought him back to Cambridge.

After his return to Cambridge, Dirac received a letter from Heisenberg, who told him about his own journey from Japan via Shanghai and Hong Kong to Germany. Heisenberg shared Dirac's interest in walking and hiking. "The best part was the trip to the biggest and best mountains," he wrote. "In India itself it was very hot and rather rainy. Once our train went off the rails in the middle of the Jungle and people were very afraid of tigers; the tigers probably were pretty afraid too." Dirac did not stay long in his room in St. John's College. Apart from several shorter visits to Europe, in the summer of 1931, he returned to the United States, this time, to give lectures at Princeton University.

Before taking up his academic duties, he spent time with his friend Van Vleck in Madison. Dirac was not used to dining in American hotels where the ice water was very cold and the soup very hot. As Van Vleck recalled, Dirac took hand of the situation "with his characteristic directness by transferring an ice cube from the water to the soup." Together with his companion Dirac hiked and camped in the Rocky Mountains. "I enjoyed myself very much in the Rockies," he wrote to

Tamm, "although I did not do any difficult mountaineering but mostly kept to the trails." Three years later, again in Van Vleck's company, he did some pretty difficult mountaineering in the Rockies, which included an ascent of the 4,360-meter (14,308-feet) Uncompagrhe Peak, the sixth highest summit of the Rocky Mountains. He subsequently went to Princeton's famous Institute for Advanced Study—where Einstein had settled the year before—and where Dirac spent two terms. However, instead of going directly back to England after his appointment at Princeton ended, he went westwards for another tour around the world. The route of this journey was largely the same as that taken five years earlier, although this time he entered the Trans-Siberian Railway at Irkutsk after having traveled through China.

At the Institute for Advanced Study in Princeton, Dirac's room was close to Einstein's but apparently the two geniuses were not in contact. This is a bit strange, especially because a year earlier Einstein had recommended Dirac for a new chair at the Institute, rating him above Pauli. On the other hand, Dirac came to know the Hungarian theoretical physicist Eugene Paul Wigner closely. Three months younger than Dirac, Wigner was originally trained in chemical engineering. More attracted by mathematical subjects, he switched to atomic and quantum physics; in these areas, he became an important part of the German physics community. However, as a Jew he had no hope of a career in Germany after 1933, so he settled in the United States and became a naturalized citizen four years later. Wigner and Dirac had first met in 1928 when Dirac gave a lecture in Göttingen. Although impressed by the content of the lecture, Wigner was surprised at Dirac's style of presentation, which he described as "detached, almost like a recitation of a technical text." Dirac spoke about the exciting new quantum field theory "without giving any sign of enjoying his own lecture."

In the fall of 1934, Wigner's younger sister Margit visited him in Princeton, where Dirac met her for the first time. Margit Wigner Balasz was divorced and had two children, Gabriel and Judith. Until that time, Dirac's relationship with women had been peripheral and platonic. He was generally thought to be an inveterate bachelor, perhaps gay and repressed. How could a woman possibly occupy a place in his mind (not to mention his heart), filled, as it was, with equations? Yet, the "genius who fears all women" (as *Sunday Dispatch* described him in 1933) eventually fell in love. Margit went back to Budapest while Dirac continued with his physics and the second world tour. However, he had not forgotten the Hungarian divorcée, whom he visited in August of 1935 on his way home from Moscow. When Dirac returned to Cambridge, he wrote Margit a letter to tell her that he missed her very much. "I do not understand why this should be, as I do not usually miss people when I leave them." Unlike the British quantum genius, Margit was talkative, passionate and extremely social. But Dirac was warming up to her, proving that opposites sometimes really do attract. It took time for Dirac to commit, but finally, on January 2, 1937, the two married.

Physicist Ernest Rutherford mistakenly believed that Margit was a widow. In a letter of early 1937, he told a friend about the surprising wedding news, commenting, "I think it will require the ability of an experienced widow to look after him adequately!" However, despite their personality differences, the marriage was happy and lasting. Paul and Margit (known as "Manci") had two daughters of their own, Mary Elizabeth and Florence Monica. Paul's stepson Gabriel studied mathematics at Cambridge University, graduating with a Ph.D. degree in 1951. He later went to work in the Mathematics Department at Aarhus University in Denmark. When he died at 59 in July of 1984, his stepfather attended the interment in Aarhus. It was Dirac's next-to-last trip. He passed away three months later in Tallahassee, Florida.

Under Margit's influence, Paul became more social. A year after their marriage, he wrote his wife a moving letter in which he gratefully admitted the change in his life that she had incited: "You have made me human. I shall be able to live happily with you even if I have no more success in my work." Although Dirac became more "human," he was not exactly ordinary. Gamow told the story of how one of Dirac's old friends, a physicist, came to see him shortly after the wedding. Unaware of the marriage, the friend was surprised to find a woman in Dirac's house. When Dirac noticed his curiosity, he said, "Oh, I'm sorry. I forgot to introduce you. This is … this is Wigner's sister."

Under Stalin's rule, the Soviet Union attracted only a few foreign scientists and almost no tourists. However, Dirac found the country most interesting and visited it no less than seven times between 1928 and 1937, the last time in the company of his wife. This was the year of what is known as the "great terror "—Stalin's bloody eradication of his enemies, real or perceived. Many of the victims were scientists, and a few of them foreigners. In a letter he penned in 1937, Kapitza mentioned that many of the theoretical physicists at Leningrad University had been arrested, charged with being enemies of the state. "In fact," Kapitza wrote, "so many were arrested that in the university faculty of mathematics and physics no one could be found to lecture to students." When Dirac wanted to visit the country yet another time in 1938, he was refused a visa.

During the 1930s, Dirac had very close relations to Soviet physicists and a genuine interest in what he, as well as many other Western scientists and intellectuals, saw as a promising social and economic experiment. Of Dirac's almost 200 publications, only four were collaborative papers and, of these, two were written with Russian co-authors. In 1931, he was elected a corresponding member of the USSR Academy of Science, a rare honor for a 29-year-old physicist and one with political overtones. On the advice of Kapitza, six years later Dirac contributed a paper to a special issue of the *Bulletin of the USSR Academy of Science* commemorating the 20th anniversary of the October Revolution. The paper could be seen as a political manifestation, but this was hardly Dirac's intention. It was of a purely scientific nature.

Although Dirac was highly regarded in the Soviet Union, his view of quantum theory did not please the new communist society's ideological guardians. To them, it smelled a little too much of bourgeois idealism. The 1932 Russian translation of *Principles of Quantum Mechanics* was supplied with a preface by the publisher warning naïve readers that the book "contains many views and statements completely at variance with dialectical materialism." Likewise, in the second edition of 1937, the publisher pointed out that Dirac "makes some philosophical and methodological generalizations that contradict the only truly scientific method of cognition—dialectical materialism."

The autumn of 1933 was busy for Dirac. First, he attended a conference in Copenhagen, and from there he proceeded to another one in Leningrad. He wanted Bohr to join him. "You may be sure of a warm welcome from the Russian physicists and I think you will find it interesting to see something of the modern Russia. (The economic situation there is completely different from everywhere else)." Dirac was impressed by the socialist experiment and took great interest in the improvements of industry, living standards, and availability of consumer goods. It did not occur to him that what he saw was only what the Soviet authorities allowed him to see.

After the Leningrad conference, Dirac participated in his third Solvay Congress in Brussels, the subject of which was the physics of atomic nuclei. In December, he was in Stockholm to receive the Nobel Prize.

Dirac and Heisenberg in Brussels, attending the 1933 Solvay Conference. Credit: Niels Bohr Archive, Copenhagen.

Following the etiquette, he gave a brief speech at the traditional Nobel banquet. It was quite unusual. Most laureates use the speech to summarize their scientific work or put it into some larger perspective, but Dirac instead dealt with the "great similarity between the problems provided by the mysterious behaviour of the atom and those provided by the present economic paradoxes confronting the world." The effects of the great economic depression were still all too visible. Undoubtedly to the surprise of the audience, Dirac argued that the cause of these troubles was "an economic system which tries to maintain an equality of value between two things, which it would be better to recognise from the beginning as of unequal value." He was referring to regular incomes versus single payments. To him, "a regular income is worth incomparably more, in fact infinitely more, in the mathematical sense, than any single payment." It is not quite clear what Dirac meant by his speech, but it might have been an allusion to the Marxist view of economy. At least, that is what Erwin Schrödinger's wife Annemarie thought. She described the speech as "a tirade of communist propaganda."

If most of the audience in Stockholm found Dirac's speculation about a similarity between quantum physics and economy to be slightly odd, his co-laureate Schrödinger did not. He gave Dirac's speech much thought and responded to it at length in a letter he wrote on Christmas Eve of 1933. In it, Schrödinger commented on a mathematical paper Dirac had recently published and which Schrödinger found hard to understand because of its brevity and condensed style. "My dear Dirac," he wrote, "one has the impression, that you are frequently afraid of using up too much paper and print. Are you not aware of the fact, that pages and pages are used up for the reproduction of thoughts, which are considerably less important than yours."

One of the physicists Dirac visited during his travels to Russia was his old friend Kapitza, who in 1934 had been prevented by the Soviet authorities from returning to Cambridge. In letters from the summer of 1935, Kapitza told about Dirac's stay with him in Bolshevo, outside Moscow. He emphasized the human traits of the great theorist: "Dirac treats me so simply and so well that I can feel what a good and loyal friend he is." In another letter: "Dirac and I get on very pleasantly together, chatting and discussing only when we feel like it. ... As always, Dirac is somewhat eccentric but I find him easy to get along with. I tried to get Dirac into a flirtation with a good looking girl at 18, who is a language student and speaks English—but I had no success."

Although Dirac's attitude to the Soviet Union and its economic system was clearly positive, he was probably not a Marxist and at no time was he a member of the communist party, or any other political party. Nevertheless, for a period, he was friendly to the economic and social system of the Soviet regime, which he tacitly endorsed and valued from a scientific and logical point of view. Dirac traveled with British socialists and communists, but in a detached and passive way only. His many travels to the Soviet Union and general sympathy for the country later got him into trouble. In 1954, for the fourth time after the war, Dirac wanted once again to visit the United States but, this time, he was denied a visa. No reason was given, but this was at the height of the Cold War, and there is little doubt that his many contacts with Soviet physicists made him suspicious in the eyes of McCarthyist circles. After vehement protests from the American scientific community, the decision was reversed.

When Britain declared war on Germany in 1939, Dirac could not completely withstand the pressure to become engaged in matters outside pure physics. British scientists investigated at an early date the possibility of constructing an atomic bomb and Dirac became involved in the work, if only peripherally and on a consultancy basis. He contributed to theoretical models of a uranium bomb and the separation of isotopes through centrifuges. This work was relatively important and highly classified. When the British bomb project was taken over by the huge Manhattan Project in the United States, the American–British group of physicists at Los Alamos wanted Dirac to join them. He refused. Dirac spent the rest of the war years in Cambridge and Dublin, where he attempted to reformulate quantum electrodynamics, a line of pure research with no connection whatsoever to military applications.

Dirac's rather sporadic involvement in war–related physics did not spring from a patriotic desire to contribute to the war efforts. What primarily motivated him to do research on uranium physics and centrifuge technology was not the military context, but the scientific relevance. Neither should his decision not to participate in the Manhattan Project be seen as a conscious opposition to using physics for military purposes. This was not a question that preoccupied Dirac. He also did not seem to have cared much about the scientists' ethical responsibility and the problems raised by the new nuclear weapons. These topics were widely discussed in the immediate post-war period, but not by Dirac. On the whole, he was the arch-typical ivory-tower scientist.

6

Against the Stream

A n independent and original thinker, Dirac never cared about the fashions of the physics community. He basically worked in fields that *he* found to be fundamental and interesting, unconcerned with whether or not they were judged to belong to mainstream physics. Or he simply invented new fields, as he did in the case of monopole and positron physics. Any idea of joining popular trends, or otherwise bending his ideas to adapt to majority views was totally foreign to him. It may have been in this connection that Bohr once remarked: "of all physicists, Dirac has the purest soul." There was a price to pay for the purity, both scientifically and socially, but Dirac was willing to pay it.

Although Dirac was not blind to the value of experimental research—on one or two occasions he even engaged in experiments—he favored methods based on pure mathematical reasoning over the more standard empirical-inductive approach. The latter method became increasingly popular after World War II when advanced apparatus (in the form of accelerators and detectors, for example) stimulated a close integration of theory and experiment. Theoretical progress relied on and was guided ever more closely by new experimental data. On the organizational side, teams involving both theoretical and experimental physicists became the rule rather than the exception. Individual research was out, and teamwork was in.

In a talk he gave in 1972, Dirac referred with regret to the then dominant method of physics, namely to "keep close to the experimental results, hear about all the latest information that the experimenters obtain and then proceed to set up a theory to account for them." This approach, he continued, "might develop somewhat into a rat-race. Of course, it needs rather intelligent rats to take part in it." As far as fundamental physics was concerned, Dirac much preferred to rely on mathematics and his own basic beliefs, without paying too much attention to experimental results. He explained: "It's just that one feels that nature is constructed in a certain way and one hangs onto the idea rather like one might hang onto a religious belief."

As Dirac did not follow the trends in method, he did not follow the trends in popularity among different subjects of physics either. At any given time, some subjects attract more students, money, and glamor than other subjects, and not necessarily for good reasons. In the first decades after the end of World War II, nuclear physics, elementary particle physics, and solid-state physics were by far the most popular and fast-growing areas of research. Dirac showed no interest in any of them. Instead, he had become fascinated with the electron and felt no need to consider the multitude of new particles discovered in the cosmic rays or in the ever more powerful high-energy accelerators. One or two elementary particles were enough for the ascetic Cambridge physicist.

Only on one occasion did Dirac consider another elementary particle, and then it was a close relative of the electron, the 207 times heavier muon. Discovered in 1936, the muon, originally called a "meson" or "mesotron," is radioactive and decays spontaneously to an electron and a neutrino. In 1962, while revising his classical theory of the electron, Dirac suggested that instead of being a point-particle, "if one supposes the electron to have a finite size, ... one can assume that the lowest excited state is the muon." On this basis, he was able to calculate the mass of the muon to 53 times the electron's mass, not an impressive agreement. The discrepancy did not worry Dirac much, as his model did not incorporate spin and thus could not be expected to correspond to a real particle. In any case, his theory of the finite-size electron and its cousin, the muon, was completely out of tune with the ideas of particle physicists at the time.

While the new generation of competitive particle physicists tended to dismiss Dirac as a cantankerous old man holding on to the past, he himself considered particle hunting as an unappealing enterprise. Dirac's preference for cultivating subjects according to his own taste led him on several occasions, and especially after the mid-1930s, into areas that were far from mainstream physics. His work on cosmology and the constants of nature was definitely unconventional, and the same was the case with much of his research related to quantum theory. On the other hand, he never crossed the fine line between science and pseudo-science.

Contrary to most of his younger colleagues, Dirac could afford the luxury of working only on subjects that pleased him. Not only was he a highly reputed Nobel laureate with few students, but he was also a theorist in no need of collaboration or input from teams of experimenters. A leading expert in general relativity characterized him as "one of the very few scientists who could work even on a lonely island if he had a library and could perhaps even do without books and journals." According to another contemporary physicist, "Dirac is a man who could never, between his great discoveries, do any sort of bread and butter problem." This was not totally accurate, but it was close enough to the truth. Dirac's view concerning mainstream physics and the methods of physics was original, but not exceptional. It was to a large extent shared by Einstein, who similarly placed himself on the sideline of mainstream science. Indeed, after about 1950, Dirac found himself in a position not unlike that of Einstein by challenging the conventional wisdom of quantum physics, both men isolated themselves. However, their objections to the state of affairs in fundamental physics were based on entirely different reasons. They had only one thing in common: they made almost no impact on the physics community.

At about the time when Dirac proposed his theory of the anti-electron, soon to become a theory of the positron, the foundation of quantum mechanics was a subject of worry to the physics community. In 1930, Bohr suggested to Dirac that "the solution to the present troubles will not be reached without a revision of our general physical ideas still deeper than that contemplated in the present quantum mechanics." The troubles that Bohr referred to related to the attempts to establish a consistent quantum theory of electromagnetic interactions—a quantum field theory—in agreement with the theory of relativity. A few years later, Oppenheimer described the situation in quantum physics more pointedly: the existing theory was simply "in a hell of a way." The responses to what was generally perceived as a crisis varied. Several prominent physicists, including Heisenberg, Pauli, and Dirac, believed that the problems could not be solved within existing theory but should be exploited in constructing a radically different theory of the future. Other physicists preferred a more conservative and pragmatic approach that would build on improvements of existing quantum theory.

To get an impression of the sense of crisis in the physics community during Dirac's lifetime, we just need to consider the electron. Although described with admirable precision by Dirac's equation of 1928, when the electron's interaction with its own field was taken into account, it behaved strangely, almost perversely. Several problems turned up, the nastiest one being that the electron's mass became infinite. Infinities are not necessarily bad news if they are of a mathematical nature only. But if they are concerned with real and measurable quantities such as the electron's mass, which obviously *cannot* be infinite, then they are bad news. Dirac had created a large part of the foundation of quantum electrodynamics and quantum field theory and naturally felt committed to the development of these areas of fundamental physics. He was no less worried about these issues than Bohr and Oppenheimer. In a valiant attempt to remedy some of the problems, he published in 1934 a complicated field theory of electrons and positrons. The theory's orgy of mathematical equations was impressive, but the infinities remained.

This was the beginning of Dirac's gradual move into non-mainstream areas of physics as far as quantum mechanics was concerned. Of course, what is defined as mainstream is a sociological and not a scientific question. In the years after 1934, Dirac focused on finding better quantum equations, improving the mathematical basis of quantum mechanics, or by some other means solving the problems that haunted existing theory. For example, whereas his relativistic wave equation of 1928 only described electrons and other possible particles with half-integral spin, in 1936 he produced a generalization that was presumably valid also for other elementary particles.

Also, the same year, Dirac, who was concerned with the riddles of the quantum theory of fields and particles, suggested abandoning the whole "so-called quantum electrodynamics." Without offering a proper alternative, he considered for a brief while to replace it with a theory in which energy was not strictly conserved. Although violation of energy conservation was restricted to atomic processes, it was a radical proposal. The law of absolute energy conservation is *very* fundamental. As a consequence of his temporal disbelief in energy conservation, he felt justified in questioning the existence of the neutrino, an elementary particle that Pauli had introduced to understand beta radioactivity without violating energy conservation. Although the neutrino was hypothetical (it was only detected in 1956), by 1936 almost all physicists accepted it as a real particle. But not Dirac, who was willing to sacrifice it along with the theory of quantum electrodynamics.

Dirac's drastic and somewhat desperate proposal was broadly criticized and within a year, he had returned to the safe ground of energy conservation. In the meantime, some physicists opposed to the Bohr-Heisenberg mainstream interpretation of quantum mechanics, prominent among them Einstein and Schrödinger, welcomed Dirac's heterodoxy. They mistakenly thought it was a revolt against the Copenhagen view of quantum mechanics. "I am very happy that one of the real adepts now argues for the abandonment of the awful 'quantum electrodynamics'," Einstein commented. However, at the time, Dirac did not really question the Copenhagen view, and he expressed no interest at all in the alternative ideas of Einstein and Schrödinger. He would eventually change his mind, but only much later.

"I really spent my life trying to find better equations for quantum electrodynamics," Dirac said in 1979, looking back on a long career in physics. Forty years earlier he thought that it might be worthwhile first to find better equations for the classical electron and then formulate the classical equations in terms of quantum mechanics. In this way, he hoped to get rid of the infinities. The result of this line of thinking was an important theory of the classical electron but not, unfortunately, one that could be successfully transformed into a quantum theory.

The classical electron theory was only one of several ideas that flowed from Dirac's fertile mind. Another idea was to reconsider the concept of probability that lies at the heart of quantum mechanics. The probability that something happens, say, that a radioactive atom decays in the next minute, is a number between zero and one. But why not extend the meaning of probability to *negative probabilities*—numbers smaller than zero? Perhaps it sounds crazy, but in 1941 Dirac presented to the Royal Society a new theory of quantum mechanics based on this idea. The ever-critical Pauli, at first, found the theory promising, but eventually reached the conclusion that it had nothing to do with the real world of physics—it was, he said, a "mathematical fiction." Neither this nor other theories brought Dirac closer to the goal, a mathematically consistent and physically sensible theory of quantum electrodynamics.

The goal was finally achieved in 1947 when two young American theorists, Richard Feynman and Julian Schwinger, developed their versions of a new formalism of quantum electrodynamics. A different and slightly earlier version of the same theory was independently proposed by Sin-Itiro Tomonaga in Japan. "Renormalization quantum electrodynamics" is a terrible name, but that is what the theory is called. In a nutshell, based on the existing framework of quantum mechanics and relativity theory, the two Americans developed schemes that allowed them to calculate measurable quantities (such as the mass of the electron) and obtain finite answers. The infinities did not really disappear in the new theory, but they were tamed in the sense that they did not show up in the final result. By means of a clever subtraction procedure, a finite number was obtained by subtracting an infinite number from another infinite number! The great advantage of the renormalization theory was that it worked. It was quickly used to make detailed calculations of experimental phenomena that hitherto had escaped explanation, and the calculations agreed impressively with data.

Dirac was not directly involved in the creation of what was heralded as a new paradigm in quantum theory, but indirectly he was—some of his early papers served as important sources of inspiration for the three founders of the paradigm. At any rate, having digested the theory, Dirac came to the conclusion that it could not possibly be correct. The hostile attitude towards renormalization quantum electrodynamics remained throughout the rest of his life. It turned him into an outsider in the science that he had done more than anyone else to create. While the new generation of quantum physicists celebrated the end of the more than decade-long war against the infinities and happily went on with their calculations, Dirac thought that the battle had been won using foul means. To him, it was not a genuine victory.

"What we need and shall strive after," Dirac said in a talk he gave in 1949, "is a change in the fundamental concepts, analogous to the change in 1925 from Bohr to Heisenberg and Schrödinger, which will sweep away the present difficulties automatically." He was too modest to mention his own role in this dramatic phase in the history of quantum physics. Dirac hoped to repeat the success of his youth when quantum mechanics had been discovered almost by accident. Relativity and quantum mechanics had been established through a series of revolutionary steps; Dirac was convinced that a new revolution was needed. The breakthrough of quantum electrodynamics in the late 1940s, on the other hand, was fundamentally conservative. It was not a radically new theory but, rather, the old theory dressed up in fancy new clothes.

At the bottom of Dirac's resistance to post-war quantum theory were questions about the meaning and values of physics. The outlook of Schwinger, Feynman, and others of the new generation of quantum physicists was pragmatic and one-sidedly focused on getting answers from theory that agreed with experiment. Physics, they said, was a matter of calculation and comparison between calculated and experimental results—no more and no less. With the new U.S. style of physics, questions that related to interpretation or even worse—to philosophy, were avoided or denigrated. Conceptual scrutiny of the foundations of physics tended to be seen as an unnecessary luxury. This attitude to fundamental physics, still popular among many modern physicists, has been summarized in the sentence "shut up and calculate!"

Dirac was not a stranger to the "shut up and calculate" philosophy, which he shared to some extent in the early part of his career. Physical theory, he said, was basically a formal instrument that allowed the calculation of experimental results. This was also the implicit message of his great textbook in quantum mechanics. One reviewer of the book paraphrased, not unfairly, Dirac's view as follows: "A mathematical machine is set up, and without asserting or believing that it is the same as Nature's machine, we put in data at one end and take out results at the other. As long as these results tally with those of Nature ... we regard the machine as a satisfactory theory." As late as 1967, in the fourth edition of *Principles of Quantum Mechanics*, Dirac subscribed to a view of this kind, effectively limiting physics to mathematical manipulations of symbols related to observable quantities. "Only questions about the results of experiments have a real significance," he wrote, "and it is only such questions that theoretical physics has to consider."

However, Dirac's attitude to the pragmatic "shut up and calculate" view changed under the impact of the disagreeable renormalization quantum theory. Along with several other physicists of the pre-war generation, Dirac disliked the new style of physics. In 1981, near the end of his life, Dirac delivered an address entitled "Does Renormalization Make Sense?" It was a rhetorical question. "Some physicists may be happy to have a set of working rules leading to results in agreement with observation," he pointed out. "They may think that this is the goal of physics. But it is not enough. One wants to understand how Nature works." To Feynman and his kindred souls understanding could be reduced to empirically successful calculations. In another address from the same period, Dirac pointed out that even a wrong theory might produce results in agreement with observation. His favorite example was the kind of atomic theory he had met in his youth—Bohr's orbital model of the atom. "The Bohr theory ... gave very good answers, but still the Bohr theory had the wrong concepts," Dirac noted. "Correspondingly, the renormalized kind of quantum theory with which physicists are working nowadays is not justifiable by agreement with experiments under certain conditions."

Dirac admitted that renormalization quantum electrodynamics was highly successful in terms of agreement between theory and experiment, but he thought that the price for the success was much too high. Not only did the theory not lead to a proper understanding of nature, but it also built on working rules without foundation in logic and what he considered to be "sensible mathematics." According to Dirac, the infinities had not disappeared, they had been neglected. "Sensible mathematics involves neglecting a quantity when it is small—not neglecting it just because it is infinitely great and you do not want it!" Dirac was not alone in criticizing the new quantum electrodynamics, but one of the recurring elements in his uncompromising opposition was particular to him. This was the emphasis of the theory's lack of aesthetical quality. Since the 1930s, Dirac had been increasingly concerned by the role of what he called "beautiful mathematics" in physics, and he could find no beauty at all in the new quantum electrodynamics. On the contrary, it was "complicated and ugly," he said.

To most practicing physicists in the post-war period, the issue of consistency in quantum theory was just a pedantic problem they did not need to address. Nor did the generation of Schwinger and Feynman appreciate the aesthetic values that Dirac and his contemporaries associated with physics. By 1950, Dirac was no longer a young man. He may have recalled the *Faust* parody staged at Bohr's Institute nearly two decades earlier, when he recited in German a passage translated into English:

> Age is, of course, a fever chill
> That every physicist must fear.
> He's better dead than living still,
> When once he's past his thirtieth year.

Or he may have recalled how he congratulated the slightly older Heisenberg on his 30th birthday: "You are now past 30 and you are no longer a physicist."

During the last decade of his life, Dirac concentrated on two separate research projects, both of which were well outside mainstream science. One was aimed at a new foundation of quantum theory, and the other was his idea that the constant of gravitation varied in time. His attempts to improve quantum theory in general and quantum electrodynamics, in particular, took many directions, some more unorthodox than others. One of them was a proposal of reintroducing the ether, the medium that had played such a predominant role in Victorian physics but vanished from the scene with the acceptance of relativity theory. However, Dirac's ether was different from the classical version as it was based on quantum mechanics and in agreement with the theory of relativity. It could not be ascribed a definite velocity and, for this reason, it did not justify the absolute space and time associated with the Newtonian world picture.

Nevertheless, Dirac considered his ether as physically real as his Victorian predecessors had done. He even speculated, much like some of the ether physicists of the *fin-de-siècle* period, that his ether might be "a very light and tenuous form of matter." Dirac thought that the new quantum ether might serve as an ally in his continual fight against the fashions of current quantum theory, but nothing useful came out of the idea. While the press showed interest in it, the physicists did not.

Indeed, none of Dirac's many alternatives were even remotely successful or attracted more than polite attention in the physics community. It seemed that the quantum wizard had lost the magic wand of his youth. As the eminent Russian theoretical physicist Lev Landau viciously quipped to a colleague in 1957, "Dirac is the greatest living physicist and he has done nothing of importance since 1930."

7

Cosmythology

In the spring of 1937, when Bohr browsed through the latest issue of the weekly journal *Nature*, his eyes stopped at a note signed P. A. M. Dirac. Gamow, who happened to be visiting the Danish physicist, recalled that a perplexed Bohr turned towards him and said, "Look what happens to people when they get married." What caused Bohr's consternation was Dirac's unorthodox proposal, based on no less unorthodox numerological reasons, of a new picture of the universe and its evolution in time. Newton's gravitational constant might not be constant, Dirac suggested, but decreased slowly in cosmic time.

Until that time, Dirac had worked almost exclusively in quantum theory and shown no interest in other branches of physics, such as astrophysics and cosmology. However, he was well acquainted with the recent advances in these fields and thus prepared to make his unexpected move from the mathematical theory of the micro-cosmos to the much less precise and more speculative theory of the macro-cosmos at its largest possible scale, the universe.

The mainstream cosmology that emerged in the 1930s built on Einstein's general theory of relativity, which, as first shown by the Belgian physicist Georges Lemaître in 1927, offered an explanation of the observationally based expansion of the universe. Four years later Lemaître (who was also a Catholic priest) went a step further, arguing that the expansion had started a finite time ago when all matter in the universe was squeezed together in a primordial "atom" of unimaginably high density. Contrary to accepted wisdom, the universe could thus be ascribed a definite age. Lemaître's hypothesis of an exploding universe was the first version of what eventually became known as the Big Bang theory, a name that was coined in 1948. Dirac, who had met Lemaître and discussed his hypothesis with him, was among the very few physicists and astronomers in the 1930s who accepted the audacious idea of a finite-age exploding universe. His 1937 *Nature* note was based on the assumption that some two billion years ago at the origin of time "all the spiral nebulae were shot out from a small region of space or perhaps from a point."

The other element in Dirac's cosmological hypothesis related to the constants of nature that enter and define the fundamental laws of physics. Examples are Planck's constant h, the gravitational constant G, the speed of light c, and the elementary charge e. Their numerical values can be measured but not be derived from theory, as Dirac knew from his work with the magnetic monopole. The values of the constants evidently depend on the chosen system of units and are in this respect arbitrary. Light moves at the speed of roughly 300,000 km per second, but if we use as a length unit the distance of the Earth from the Sun, the figure shrinks to 0.002. The *dimensionless combinations* of natural constants are not subject to this kind of arbitrariness because they include no units. For example, the ratio of the proton's mass to the mass of the electron is 1836, a pure number. The fine-structure constant $\alpha = 0.0073$ is another example.

While Eddington and a few other physicists had previously considered numbers of this kind and proposed to connect them, Dirac was interested in the exceedingly large numbers. One of these dimensionless numbers, well known at the time, is the ratio between the electrical and the gravitational forces acting between a proton and an electron. Since gravity and the electrical force vary with distance in exactly the same way, the ratio is independent of the distance between the two particles. It is a huge number, about 10^{39}. Dirac then considered the age of the universe, not in years but in the much smaller and more fundamental units of "atomic time," as given by a combination of the speed of light and the electron's mass and charge (more precisely e^2/mc^3). An atomic time unit corresponds to the time it takes light to pass an atomic nucleus. The result again becomes 10^{39}, at least approximately. What a curious coincidence! Or could it be more than just a coincidence? Dirac was convinced that the near equality of the two numbers expressed one of nature's deep secrets.

From this conviction—and it was nothing but—Dirac concluded that the gravitational constant must be related to the age of the universe. More specifically, G must vary inversely with the time elapsed since the Big Bang, which we can write as $G \sim 1/t$. In the past, gravity was thus greater than today and in the future it will become smaller. Although the variation is very slow, what matters is that G is no longer a true constant as had been taken for granted since the days of Newton, and been taken over by Einstein's theory of gravitation. It was a radical hypothesis indeed. And this was not all, for applying similar numerological arguments Dirac further suggested that the number N of elementary particles in the visible universe must increase with the age—in this case as $N \sim t^2$. As the universe expands and grows older, particles will be created continuously and spontaneously, apparently contradicting the fundamental law of energy conservation.

Not afraid of generalizing, in his paper of 1937 Dirac proposed what he called the Fundamental Principle, better known as the *Large Numbers Hypothesis* (LNH), a term he first used in 1972. According to one version of the principle, when two very large numbers of the order 10^{39} or its square 10^{78} occur in nature, they must be related by a simple mathematical relation. The following year Dirac developed his hypothesis into a proper cosmological theory, although he decided to forget about matter creation and keep only the $G(t)$ hypothesis, meaning the decrease of G according to $G \sim 1/t$.

Whether in cosmology or some other branch of science, a scientific theory must have consequences that can be tested either directly or indirectly. Dirac's theory had, at least, two consequences, which distinguished it from other models of the universe. First, it followed directly from the $G(t)$ hypothesis, that relative to its current value, G should decrease at a rate of only 10^{-10} per year, or one part in ten billion years. This was a testable consequence if perhaps more in principle than in practice. The second consequence was more problematic. Dirac's model accounted for the expansion, but at a slow rate that corresponded to an embarrassingly small age of the universe—just 700 million years, or considerably less than the age of the Earth! One might think that this calculation alone ruled out the model, but according to Dirac, it might be possible to account for the glaring contradiction between theory and fact.

Dirac knew that his cosmological theory was methodologically unorthodox and empirically weak. He realized that the $G(t)$ hypothesis was incompatible with Einstein's general theory of relativity, which he greatly admired. Nonetheless, his faith in the LNH overshadowed whatever doubts he might have had. In a lecture in Edinburgh in early 1939, he imagined that the mysteries of the universe might ultimately find their explanation in terms of the large whole numbers such as 10^{39}. "Might it not be," he suggested, "that all present events correspond to properties of this large number, and, more generally, that the whole history of the universe corresponds to properties of the whole sequence of natural numbers?" Not only might the law of gravity change with time, but *all* the laws of physics might turn out to be evolutionary:

"At the beginning of time the laws of Nature were probably very different from what they are now. Thus, we should consider the laws of Nature as continually changing with the epoch, instead of as holding uniformly throughout all space-time."

As if this were not radical enough, Dirac went on to speculate that the laws of nature might also depend on position in space, meaning, for example, that the laws of electromagnetism valid in the Andromeda Galaxy are not quite the same as the laws we know here on Earth. His reason for the unusual suggestion was that one could in this way "preserve the beautiful idea of relativity that there is a fundamental similarity between space and time." But it was just a speculation. Dirac was wise enough not to return to it.

Dirac's cosmological theory of 1938, at first, attracted little scientific interest among physicists and even less so among astronomers. Eddington dismissed it as "unnecessarily complicated and fantastic." With only five citations in the period between 1938 and 1947, it was unsuccessful, at least as seen from a sociological perspective. Dirac could not possibly have foreseen the rich and diverse literature his theory would eventually give rise to.

From a more philosophical perspective, it was heavily criticized by Herbert Dingle, a British astrophysicist and philosopher of science, who accused Dirac of having betrayed the true spirit of science. "Instead of the induction of principles from phenomena," he thundered, "we are given a pseudo-science of invertebrate cosmythology, and invited to commit suicide to avoid the need of dying." In a subsequent round of discussion in the journal *Nature*, Dirac sought to avoid philosophical issues and merely restated the main points of his theory.

Uncomfortable with public debate, he somewhat lamely answered that his LNH built on the constants of nature as given by observation, and, for this reason, lived up to the standards of empirical science. Dingle disagreed. He deplored that the great Dirac had fallen victim to rationalist intoxication: "I cited Prof. Dirac's letter not as a source of infection but as an example of the bacteria which can flourish in the poisoned atmosphere; in a pure environment it would not have come to birth, and we should still have the old, incomparable Dirac."

Philosophy apart, the impossibly low age of Dirac's universe made it unpalatable to all astronomers and physicists (except Dirac himself, of course). The question of varying gravity was different, for it could be evaluated independently of the cosmological model and confronted with empirical data. In 1948, the Hungarian-American nuclear physicist Edward Teller pointed out that if G varied as predicted, it would have severe consequences for the history of the Earth. For the first time, paleontology was used to test a theory of the universe. This was possible because the luminosity of the Sun and its distance from the Earth depend on the value of G. The two effects taken together control the surface temperature of the Earth. If G were larger in the past, the Earth's climate would have been considerably warmer than it is today. Based on a rough calculation, Teller inferred that on Dirac's hypothesis the temperature in the Cambrian era, some 300 million years ago, would have been slightly above the boiling point of water. The result obviously conflicted with paleontological evidence of a rich marine life in the Cambrian, including trilobites and much more. Teller felt forced to conclude that Dirac's hypothesis was probably wrong. Most scientists agreed.

It is uncertain how Dirac reacted to Teller's objection, but apparently he was unable to come up with a satisfactory answer to it. For this reason, among others, he chose to stay out of cosmology for no less than 35 years, returning to the subject only in 1973. Yet, during this long period of silence, he maintained his belief in the $G(t)$ hypothesis, which he felt was a necessary consequence of the beautiful LNH. The predicted rate of decrease depended on the so-called Hubble time, which Dirac had originally and in accordance with astronomical observations taken to be about two billion years. The Hubble time is proportional to and of the same order as the age of the universe, the precise relationship between the two quantities depending on the chosen cosmological model. In the mid–1950s, it turned out that the Hubble time and therefore also the age of the universe was much larger than assumed.

The new and better estimate gave a rate of decrease of G that made Teller's paleoclimatic argument less serious. It would still be very warm in the Cambrian period, but not so warm that life could not survive. Dirac discussed the new situation in correspondence with Gamow, arguing that his pet hypothesis was still viable. In a letter of 1961, he wrote: "It was a difficulty with my varying gravitational constant that the time scale appeared too short, but I always believed the idea was essentially correct. Now that the difficulty is removed, of course I believe more than ever." Dirac maintained this *belief* to the end of his life.

Gamow valued Dirac's LNH but not his varying-G hypothesis, which he thought contradicted empirical knowledge. The climate in the past was far from the only problem, for there were astrophysical and geophysical problems as well. For example, calculations showed that, with a greater G in the past, the Sun would burn too fast and run out of hydrogen fuel within a period of just two billion years. We know this did not happen! When confronted with this and other difficulties Dirac sought to evade them, either by utilizing *ad hoc* hypotheses or simply by denying that the alleged difficulties were real. Gamow tried patiently to make him change his mind, but his empirical and methodological arguments fell on deaf ears. In a 1967 letter, Gamow wrote that he had "healthy respect for observation and experiment in my brain," indirectly suggesting that the brain of his friend Dirac did not possess the same healthy respect.

It is quite clear from the Dirac-Gamow correspondence that Dirac at no time seriously considered to abandon the G(*t*) hypothesis. He had, once and for all, decided that it followed uniquely from the LNH and, therefore, was correct. Dirac's dogmatic defense of the hypothesis not only featured prominently in his private correspondence, but the same kind of attitude also appeared in his publications on cosmology in the 1970s.

Most physicists and astronomers ignored Dirac's cosmological ideas, but not all did. During the long period when Dirac remained silent the G(*t*) hypothesis was advocated and further developed by Jordan in Germany, who in a general way shared many of the research interests of his colleague in Cambridge. Jordan was an early convert to Lemaître's exploding universe, which he endorsed in a book published in 1936. When Dirac suggested his cosmology-based LNH, Jordan eagerly took it up and developed it in his own way. In 1952, he rightly pointed out that, "I am the only one who has been ready to take Dirac's world model seriously … and to consider its more precise formulation." He described Dirac's LNH and the resulting G(*t*) hypothesis as "one of the great insights of our time," a view not shared by other physicists. Jordan went considerably further than Dirac by applying the hypothesis not only to astrophysics and cosmology, but also to geophysics.

From about 1955 to 1970, Dirac's hypothesis of weakening gravitation was referred to in the geological literature more frequently than in papers and books on cosmology. In the 1965 edition of his authoritative textbook *Principles of Geophysics*, Arthur Holmes, a highly reputed British geologist, referred favorably to the idea that "the universal constant of gravitation, G, may have decreased with time, as inferred by P. A. M. Dirac in 1938." This was the period in which

Dirac, seated in the front row between Aage Bohr and Otto Frisch, at the 1963 Niels Bohr commemoration conference in Copenhagen. Heisenberg is no. 4 from the right, and Jordan stands at the left in the second row. Credit: Niels Bohr Archive, Copenhagen.

Alfred Wegener's controversial hypothesis of drifting continents was revived and turned into the modern theory of plate tectonics. In this process, some earth scientists suggested, the Earth was expanding, thereby making the continents spread apart. Jordan and several others argued that the mechanism causing the expansion was Dirac's decreasing gravity. In 1971, Jordan published a monograph titled *The Expanding Earth*, characteristically subtitled *Some Consequences of Dirac's Gravitation Hypothesis*.

Dirac was aware of the expanding Earth hypothesis and its connection to his own $G(t)$ hypothesis, but he had little interest in geology and, with a few exceptions, took no part in the discussion. And perhaps wisely so, for by the early 1970s the expanding Earth theory was abandoned by the large majority of earth scientists who instead joined the new paradigm of plate tectonics. The hypothesis of a varying G was unorthodox, but about 1970, it attracted nonetheless considerable interest and was taken up by other scientists. One of them was Fred Hoyle, the famous Cambridge physicist and cosmologist, who used to be one of the very few Ph.D. students supervised by Dirac. In the early 1970s, Hoyle suggested a new theory of gravitation, which led to the same result as Dirac's hypothesis—a slowly decreasing gravitational constant. However, Hoyle's theory did not rely on the LNH.

In 1973, Dirac finally returned to his cosmological $G(t)$ theory, although now in its original formulation that included matter creation increasing with the square of cosmic time. He vaguely described the spontaneous creation of matter as "a new physical process, a kind of radioactivity, which is quite different from all the observed radioactivity." There were two possibilities for matter creation, he explained. Either new matter might be created uniformly throughout the universe ("additive creation") and therefore mostly in intergalactic regions; or it might be created at places where there already was a high concentration of matter, as in stars and planets ("multiplicative creation"). Dirac generally preferred multiplicative creation because it clashed less violently with general relativity. Whether creation occurred in one way or the other, G would decrease slowly at about the same rate as in his old theory. On the positive side, the age problem that had plagued his original theory disappeared, for Dirac's model of the 1970s implied an age of the universe as high as 18 billion years.

In a rare comment on the geologists' discussions about the history of the Earth, Dirac supported the idea of an expanding Earth, which he ascribed to matter creation and not to decreasing gravity: "According to the present theory the earth must have been expanding during geological times, owing to the continual creation of new matter inside it. The observed drifting apart of the continents supports this view." Dirac realized that the matter creation hypothesis was problematic in several respects, but although he noted the problems, he apparently did not take them very seriously. For example, in 1973, he pointed out that if atoms had multiplied during geological time, it was hard to understand why it did not have an effect on the growth of crystals. This, he said, "might lead to insuperable difficulties." After this comment, he gave up on the problem. Again, in which form was the new matter created? How was it that the continuous creation process mysteriously reproduced the chemical composition of matter already existing? Dirac provided no answer.

The new theory was not very successful. Not only was it based on the empirically unsupported hypothesis of gravitation decreasing in time, but it was also unable to explain the cosmic microwave background without special and rather implausible assumptions. The new Big Bang model of the universe that arose in the 1960s rested on two empirical foundations. The one was the successful explanation of the background radiation as a fossil of the Big Bang, and the other was the explanation of the large amount of helium in the universe. Dirac's $G(t)$ cosmology could offer no satisfactory answer to either of the phenomena, which naturally caused cosmologists in the new mainstream tradition to look at it with suspicion. After having examined Dirac's theory, one of the mainstream cosmologists at Yale University, Gary Steigman, concluded: "The application of the LNH to physics and cosmology is fraught with ambiguity." What he meant was that this kind of cosmology should not have been taken seriously.

Dirac listened to the criticism, but it did not sway him. He was convinced that, in the end, the LNH and the $G(t)$ hypothesis derived from it would prove right, that is, be in agreement with experimental evidence. The crucial test would consist of measurements of the gravitational constant, which either proved or disproved that G varied at the predicted rate. Dozens of measurements and arguments of this kind were discussed in the 1960s and 1970s, but they all turned out to be as inconclusive as Teller's old argument based on the climate of the ancient Earth. Precise astronomical measurements that could directly detect a variation in the gravitational force were needed.

Based on observations of this kind, Thomas Van Flandern, an American astronomer, announced in 1975 that he had found strong evidence for a gravitational constant decreasing in accordance with Dirac's prediction. Dirac, who was in contact with Van Flandern, thought for a while that his hypothesis had now finally been confirmed. However, Van Flandern's sensational announcement turned out to be premature. The optimistic conclusion was soon challenged by more precise data from the Viking landers on Mars. Based on more than 1,000 measurements of the Earth–Mars distance between 1976 and 1982, astrophysicist Ronald Hellings and his collaborators got results that squarely contradicted Dirac's variation prediction. Commenting on the paper by the American team, *New Scientist* spelled out its findings in plain words: "Gravity does not vary in time."

Eighty-one-year-old Dirac was informed of this conclusion, but it did not shake his belief that G decreased in time in agreement with the LNH. He believed that the experiments, not the theory, were flawed. As Dirac recalled, when Einstein proposed in 1905 that, based on his theory of relativity, electrons gained mass when moving at high speed, experiments at first proved his prediction wrong. But Einstein insisted that the theory was correct and that the experimental result was unreliable. He was right, for improved techniques changed the verdict from refuted to confirmed. Dirac thought that history would repeat itself, and his theories would be found to be correct as well.

But history rarely repeats itself in exactly the same way, and, in this case, it did not. Today it is known that if G varies, it does so at a rate much slower than Dirac predicted. By the very nature of things—or rather by the inevitable error margins of all measurements—it can never be proved experimentally that G does not change *at all.*

So, whether Dirac liked it or not, the hypothesis that he so firmly believed in for more than 30 years was just wrong. And yet, his work on the LNH and its consequences was more than just a failed excursion into cosmythology, a chapter in the history of physical thought that should better be forgotten. This work gave rise to much research in the constants of nature and their possible variation in time, areas of research that are still cultivated by physicists. Even though Dirac's $G(t)$ is dead, his LNH is not. It is a principle that continues to be explored by some physicists. Dirac's paper of 1937, in which he introduced the LNH concept, has received a total of 1,360 citations in the scientific literature. More than half of the citations were made after his death.

One reason for the continued appeal of the LNH is related to the recent interest in the so-called anthropic principle, the general claim that the constants of nature and the laws of physics are "designed" to allow the existence of intelligent carbon-based life in the universe. The roots of the much-discussed anthropic principle go back to the early 1960s, when the American physicist Robert Dicke reconsidered the meaning of Dirac's LNH, arguing that the large numbers 10^{39} and 10^{78} were conditioned by biological factors. He thought that Dirac was wrong in implicitly assuming that the epoch of humans was random. According to Dicke, the present value of the age of the universe—that is, 10^{39} in atomic time units—should be understood as a consequence of the existence of habitable planets with human life. Dicke's argument generated a characteristically brief reply from Dirac, who pointed out that if Dicke were right, humans could exist only for a limited period: "With my assumption," he noted, "they could exist indefinitely in the future and life need never end. There is no decisive argument for deciding between these assumptions. I prefer the one that allows the possibility of endless life."

This was more than just a casual remark. Dirac sincerely believed that human life in the universe could never come to an end, or, rather, that it *must* not come to an end. Far from being a deduction from science, it was an "article of faith" for him, as he wrote in private notes from 1933. It was "an assumption that I must make for my peace of mind." To Dirac, as to most believers in eternal life, it was not only a question of preserving life, but also of securing an "endless chain of progress." It was not a new theme in science, for none other than Charles Darwin had said the same when faced with the consequences of the "heat death" as predicted by the physicists' law of irreversible entropy increase. It was, Darwin said, an "intolerable thought" that humans and "all other sentient beings are doomed to complete annihilation after such long-continued slow progress." It is unlikely that Dirac knew of Darwin's autobiography, but he definitely agreed with the emotional desire of the illustrious naturalist.

At about the time of Dirac's death, the theme of eternal life was taken up by a few physicists and astronomers who have developed it into the branch of science sometimes known as "physical eschatology." Dirac would probably not have found the work of the new physical eschatologists attractive. For him, endless life was an emotional desideratum, not something that needed scientific justification.

8

Natural Philosopher

It may sound strange to refer to Dirac as a natural philosopher, a term with a curiously archaic ring to it. But until the beginning of the 20th century, British physicists often preferred their field to be called "natural philosophy" rather than "physics." Dirac's predecessor in the Lucasian chair, Joseph Larmor, was of the old school and thought of himself as a natural philosopher rather than a physicist. When Max Born became professor of physics at the University of Edinburgh in 1936, his title was Professor of Natural Philosophy. One of Dirac's first papers, a note on "The Relativity Dynamics of a Particle," was published in 1924 in the *Philosophical Magazine*, a distinguished journal of physics founded in 1788. So Paul Dirac could rightly be called a natural philosopher, at least of a kind. But he was definitely not a philosopher in the conventional sense, and he never fancied himself as one. In fact, he was plainly uninterested in philosophy, a subject of which he had only the most superficial knowledge and was never tempted to take up for serious study.

As an engineering student in Bristol, 18-year-old Dirac listened to Broad's lectures on the philosophical aspects of relativity theory, which induced him to do some reading in philosophy. What he read did not appeal to him, and he soon came to the conclusion that philosophy was merely an unimportant play with words. He felt, as he stated later in life, "that all the things that philosophers said were rather indefinite, and [I] came to the conclusion eventually that I did not think philosophy could contribute anything to the advance of physics." This was a view that stayed with Dirac throughout his life. In a 1963 interview, he put it this way: "I feel that philosophy will never lead to important discoveries. It's just a way of talking about discoveries which have already been made." Notice that for Dirac philosophy could only be of value if it served physicists in their theories and experiments. He did not appreciate that there might be other reasons to take philosophy seriously.

Dirac's attitude to philosophy, more indifferent than hostile, was not shared by many of his continental colleagues. Physicists such as Schrödinger and Heisenberg, not to mention Einstein and Bohr, were deeply interested in philosophical questions and not only in those that were considered scientifically useful. On the other hand, Dirac's attitude was far from exceptional. "Philosophy of science is as useful to scientists as ornithology is to birds," Feynman is supposed to have said. Never mind if the quotation is apocryphal (which it is), it expresses a view shared by many physicists, including Dirac. Nevertheless, philosophical considerations—in the vague meaning of considerations that go beyond measurement and calculation—were not absent from his science. There is, in fact, a good deal of implicit or spontaneous philosophy in Dirac's writings, ideas of a philosophical kind that grew out of his physics. For example, the Large Numbers Hypothesis (LNH) was partly of a philosophical nature. Although certain consequences of the LNH can be tested, such as a varying gravitational constant, the LNH itself can neither be tested nor derived from the laws of physics. It is a *belief* beyond the range of science.

Recall Dirac's prediction of magnetic monopoles in 1931. Dirac proved that, under certain circumstances, monopoles *could* exist according to the laws of electrodynamics and quantum mechanics. But do they actually exist? Dirac thought they did, his sole argument being that "one would be surprised if Nature had made no use of it," namely, turned the possibility into a reality. Without reflecting on the nature of his argument, in effect, he postulated that there is a close correlation between potential and actual existence. And more than that, because the former kind of existence *requires* the latter. If an entity is allowed to exist, meaning that it does not violate any of the fundamental laws of nature, then it does exist. This kind of argument, or rather belief, was of a *philosophical* nature since it could not be justified by either experiment or theory. Dirac may not have been aware that he argued as a philosopher, but in fact, he did.

When the monopole began to attract attention in the physics community and experimentalists started to hunt for the mysterious magnetic counterpart to the electron, the argument was sometimes stated in more explicit and elaborate forms. Thus, in a popular 1963 paper on monopoles, we read: "One of the elementary rules of nature is that, in the absence of law prohibiting an event or phenomenon it is bound to occur with some degree of probability. To put it simply and crudely: Anything that *can* happen *does* happen. Hence physicists must assume that the magnetic monopole exists unless they can find a law barring its existence." Another and shorter version that physicists are fond of is, "anything which is not prohibited is compulsory."

The argument used rather casually by Dirac in 1931 has a long and dignified past in the history of ideas where it was extensively discussed by philosophers and theologians centuries before it entered the physical sciences. Known as the *principle of plenitude*, in its modern version, it goes back principally to the great German philosopher and mathematician Gottfried Wilhelm Leibniz. When physicists today believe in the existence of black holes, gravitational waves, supersymmetric elementary particles, other universes, and superstrings, it may be because there is some observational evidence for the entities; but a stronger reason for this belief is that they can be described consistently by the laws of physics. High-energy physicists were convinced that the Higgs particle existed many years before it was detected in 2012. It just *had to* exist. The principle of plenitude is well and alive.

At about the same time that Dirac suggested the monopole, he applied similar reasoning in his interpretation of the negative-energy solutions appearing in his relativistic wave equation of 1928. The two extra variables that turned up in his wave function had to correspond to something physical. They couldn't be just mathematical symbols without physical referents. Dirac was inclined to think that the *potential* existence of positive electrons implied that they actually existed, meaning that they were inhabitants of the real world that physicists investigated. In all probability, he had never heard of the philosophical principle of plenitude. But in his 1931 paper, he referred to a somewhat similar principle suggested by Eddington as a means of establishing relations between mathematical and physical quantities appearing in general relativity theory. Dirac adopted Eddington's principle in a wider form, as a realist interpretation of mathematical quantities in terms of physical entities.

Apart from his work on monopoles and positrons, Dirac also applied a kind of plenitude reasoning in 1941 when he proposed a new version of quantum theory based on the counterintuitive notion of negative transition probabilities. Rather than dismissing such transitions between quantum states as non-existent, he wanted to interpret them physically. "Negative energies and probabilities should not be considered as nonsense," he said, pointing out that "they are well-defined concepts mathematically, like a negative sum of money." On the other hand, Dirac did not believe that just because a concept was mathematically well-defined it would be present in nature in some form or another. The negative probabilities "should be considered simply as things which do not appear in experimental results," he noted. If they did not appear in experiments, then where did they appear? According to Dirac, they belonged to a "hypothetical world" with properties that could tell the physicist something about the real world to which experiments were limited.

Dirac was aware that not *all* mathematical terms that appeared in a physical theory could be ascribed a physical meaning. After all, mathematics is immensely greater than physics, including an infinity of structures and symbols that cannot possibly have any counterpart in nature. What about a space with an infinite number of dimensions? There is a lot of difference between the claim that "the whole of the description of the universe has its mathematical counterpart," as Dirac said in 1939, and the claim that the whole of mathematics has its physical counterpart. Dirac never went as far as some modern physicists who have seriously suggested that there was a one-to-one correspondence between mathematics and physics—in other words, everything that exists mathematically also exists physically. This kind of mathematical metaphysics did not appeal to Dirac. But he thought that mathematical relations with a high degree of *beauty* were likely also to represent something real in nature. His implicit use of the principle of plenitude was guided by an even more powerful principle, what he sometimes referred to as the principle of mathematical beauty.

It is not surprising that Dirac was a believer in unity, namely, that in the last resort, nature consists of very few basis entities, which can be understood in terms of very few basic laws. This is a credo common to the large majority of physicists. The belief that nature, despite its confusing diversity, is made up of just a single entity in different disguises has been a powerful—if sometimes deceitful—guiding theme throughout history, from the atoms of the ancient Greeks to the superstrings of modern mathematical physics.

This belief influenced Dirac's thinking when he was looking for a candidate for the hypothetical positive electron and at first proposed the proton. In this way, he would "have all matter built up from one fundamental kind of particle," a result that appealed greatly to him. It would have been much nicer with just one elementary particle than two of them. Two is also a small number, but it is not aesthetically pleasing in the same way as one. In 1933, Dirac and most other physicists had accepted the neutron as a new constituent of the atomic nucleus. At the Solvay Congress that year, he suggested that the nucleus, in addition to protons and neutrons, also contained electrons.

He had no problem with this more crowded picture of the nucleus. His curious argument was that "this number [three] may appear to be large, but, from this viewpoint, two is already a large number."

The unity of nature may refer to its constituents, but it may also refer to the methods, laws and equations by means of which nature is understood. Dirac firmly believed that all of nature should be subject to the same mathematical treatment. In 1939, he used this version of nature's unity to provide an argument against the determinism of classical mechanics that was quite independent of quantum mechanics. Classical or Newtonian mechanics was a powerful theory that Dirac much admired, but it was "very unsatisfactory philosophically, as it goes against all ideas of the Unity of Nature," he said. Dirac's reasoning was that in a problem of classical mechanics the equations of motion were in a mathematical form, while the initial conditions were not. A freely falling body was governed by Galileo's law, but we could only tell what the speed of the body had been at some point in space if we knew where it started and what its initial velocity was. And the initial conditions were not subject to any law. In this way, Dirac suggested, an unpleasant asymmetry arose in the classical description of nature, separating it from one sphere ruled by mathematics and another sphere where mathematics did not apply. This he found intolerable because it ran contrary to the expectation of unity in nature.

Dirac's dream, as he exposed it in his 1939 lecture, was that ultimately *all* of nature, including initial conditions, elementary particles and constants of nature, should be amenable to mathematical analysis. In Dirac's philosophical vision, the physicist of the future would be able to deduce everything in the universe by pure mathematical reasoning. He would be omniscient, as God: "A person with a complete knowledge of mathematics could deduce, not only astronomical data, but also all the historical events that take place in the world, even the most trivial ones."

More realistically, Dirac's concern for the unity of nature—or rather the unity of physics—showed itself in his response to the so-called S-matrix theory, which in the 1960s was a popular alternative to quantum field theory. However, it was primarily a theory of nuclear forces and did not describe electrons, for example. Although S-matrix theory built on a foundation that Dirac in many ways agreed with, he nonetheless found the theory to be unattractive. His principal objection was that it destroyed the unity of physics. "We have reason to think of physics as a whole and we need to have the same underlying basis for the whole of physical theory," he wrote in 1969. And three years earlier: "In physics one should aim at a comprehensive scheme for the description of the whole of Nature. … It is necessary that quantum field theory be based on concepts and methods that can be unified with those used in the rest of physics."

While Dirac was in favor of unity in terms of concepts and methods, he remained skeptical concerning ambitious attempts at constructing a final and grand unified synthesis of all of physics. The general idea of this kind of theory is to find an equation or a system of equations that encompass and unify all the laws of physics, including quantum mechanics and general relativity. Such an ultimate theory cannot be derived from a still deeper theory—if it could, it would not be ultimate. The dream still attracts considerable interest among modern physicists who refer to it as the Theory of Everything (TOE), a name that was coined in 1985. The idea, however, is old. During Dirac's career it was pursued by, among others, Eddington, Heisenberg, and the great German mathematician David Hilbert. Dirac did not believe in a theory of everything but thought that the secrets of nature would only be revealed by gradually improving and criticizing existing theories. He likened the process to biological evolution, although one where mutations played an important role. First of all, fundamental changes would have to follow equally fundamental changes in the mathematical framework of physics. These changes would mutate indefinitely.

In the fourth, 1958 edition of *Principles of Quantum Mechanics*, Dirac criticized "from general philosophical grounds" the underlying reductionist attempts at constructing an ultimate theory of matter. Ordinary matter consists of atoms, which are built up of electrons and nuclei; the nuclei are combinations of protons and neutrons, and both of these nuclear particles consist of tightly bounds quarks. But why shouldn't electrons and quarks consist of even more fundamental particles? As Dirac argued, this kind of classical reductionist thinking was hopeless because it led to an infinite regress: "It becomes necessary to postulate that each constituent part is itself made up of smaller parts, in terms of which its behaviour is to be explained," he wrote. "There is clearly no end to this procedure, so that one can never arrive at the ultimate structure of matter on these lines."

Since the 1920s, the interpretation of quantum mechanics has attracted an enormous amount of attention among physicists as well as philosophers. Publications on the subject can easily fill a medium-sized library. As noted in Chapter 2, Dirac was not much involved in the debate over the quantum world that occurred in the 1920s and 1930s, but he largely agreed with the mainstream views of Bohr, Heisenberg, and Pauli. When Heisenberg created the basic framework of quantum mechanics in 1925, he was inspired by the semi-philosophical idea that the new theory should contain only relations between observable quantities. Impressed by what he sometimes referred to as "Heisenberg's principle," Dirac praised it on several occasions.

One version of Heisenberg's observability principle implies that quantities that are not observable do not belong to the physical world. In a few cases, Dirac used this crude version to rule out the existence of entities, arguing that they could not be observed either in principle or in practice. For example, in 1936, he dismissed the neutrino on this basis. Dirac was no less off target in 1962 when he used similar reasoning to exclude the interior of black holes from the realm of physics. At the time, he worked on problems of general relativity and at a meeting of the Royal Society he discussed some of his results. The mysterious black holes—the name "black hole" was only coined five years later—attracted much interest among physicists trying to understand and further develop Einstein's theory of gravitation. Dirac knew that the interior of a black hole could be described mathematically, but also that a signal emitted from the interior would never escape the black hole. Hence, the interior was unobservable and for this reason, Dirac concluded that it "must belong to a different universe and not be taken into account in any physical theory." He was as wrong in this case as he was in the case of the neutrino. Although black holes have not been detected in the same direct way as neutrinos, in a more indirect way they have been observed. Even the interior of a black hole is no longer considered unobservable in principle.

In most other cases, Dirac did not apply the observability principle in this rigorous way. On the contrary, he often proposed quantities that had only the slightest connection to experimental results, such as quantum states with negative energy. Despite his rhetoric, Dirac realized that the division between observables and non–observables was not given by nature alone, but also by theory. "There must be unobservable quantities coming into the theory and the hard thing is to find what these unobservable quantities are," he concluded in a paper of 1973.

In his later years, Dirac often expressed views about the quantum world, which not only differed from those he had held earlier, but also were at odds with the ideas entertained by the majority of physicists. One of the cornerstones of quantum physics is Heisenberg's

Dirac in conversation with Aage Bohr, Niels Bohr's son and a physics Nobel laureate of 1975. The occasion was the Niels Bohr commemoration meeting held in Copenhagen 1963. Photographer: John Stær. Credit: Niels Bohr Archive, Copenhagen.

uncertainty principle, as given by the formula $\Delta q \Delta p \sim h$. The validity of Heisenberg's principle, admitted even by Einstein, presupposes that Planck's constant h is absolute and fundamental. Yet in 1963, Dirac questioned the unquestionable, proposing that h might in some way be derived from the elementary charge e and the speed of light c. There is little doubt that the radical proposal was related to his cosmological ideas based on the constants of nature. At any rate, if h is not fundamental, it seems to follow that the uncertainty relations are not fundamental either. "I think one can make a safe guess that uncertainty relations in their present form will not survive in the physics of the future," he suggested. It was not, perhaps, a safe guess, but it was daring. Dirac continued to doubt the fundamental nature of Heisenberg's principle. In a 1976 lecture, he denied that it was really a cornerstone of quantum mechanics, arguing that "it is not a precise equation, but only a statement about indeterminacies."

While Dirac had almost nothing to say about the Bohr-Einstein debate in the 1930s, later on, he did refer to it in a surprising way, given his earlier allegiance to the ideas of the Copenhagen school. "My own belief was that Einstein was basically right, but he did not have a sufficiently general mathematical basis," he wrote in unpublished notes from 1974, apparently referring to his view in the 1930s. Five years later, he made it clear that his allegiance was to Einstein rather than Bohr. According to Dirac, quantum mechanics was not in its final form, such as indicated by the infinity problems of quantum electrodynamics. "The new quantum mechanics will have determinism in the way Einstein wanted," he noted. Then he added: "I think it is very likely, or at any rate quite possible, that in the long run Einstein will turn out to be correct." When he suggested that determinism would return in fundamental physics, Dirac did not have in mind the determinism of classical mechanics, but some new form of determinism the nature of which was still unknown.

Dirac never elaborated in a systematic manner his half-baked ideas concerning the interpretation of quantum mechanics. His interest in the issue was sporadic and on a level quite different from the detailed arguments of, for example, Bohr, Heisenberg, and Schrödinger. It seems that the subject did not *really* interest him. In one of his last papers, he said, revealingly, "I don't want to discuss this question of the interpretation of quantum mechanics ... I want to deal with more fundamental things." Clearly, Dirac was not a quantum philosopher.

He did share with Einstein (and several other physicists) the view that there are no final theories in physics. Quantum mechanics and general relativity were no exceptions. This had not always been his view; in his younger days, impressed by the apparently endless victories of quantum mechanics, he tended to believe that physics was approaching completeness, at least in principle. In the introduction to a paper he wrote in 1929 dealing with the application of quantum mechanics to atoms with many electrons, Dirac noted that "The general theory of quantum mechanics is now almost complete." He then proceeded to say: "The underlying physical laws necessary for the mathematical theory of a large part of physics and the whole of chemistry are thus completely known." The whole of chemistry! Dirac's reductionist declaration was not kindly received by chemists of the old school, who considered it one more proof of the theoretical physicists' arrogance and disciplinary imperialism. But it soon became part of the view adopted by the young generation of chemists who eagerly and successfully sought to turn quantum mechanics into a resource for their own science. By the mid-1930s, quantum chemistry was a reality.

The second edition of Newton's masterwork, *Principia,* stated that "to treat of God from phenomena is certainly a part of natural philosophy." Recall that "natural philosophy" means physics. Newton's 20th-century successor, Dirac was far from inspired by religious feelings just vaguely similar to those held by the former Lucasian professor. He was not a religious man and had little understanding of the cause and nature of religion. At least in his younger days, he seemed to have favored an atheistic or perhaps agnostic view, if he felt religion to be a worthy subject at all. In his memoirs, Heisenberg mentioned an informal discussion between Dirac and a couple of other physicists during the 1927 Solvay Congress. On this occasion, Heisenberg wrote, Dirac showed himself to be a "fanatic of rationalism," who considered religion to be merely a system of myths and God just an invention of the clergy. Religious ideas could not possibly appeal to the man of science. Religion and science were opposites and necessarily in conflict. Having listened to Dirac's militant atheism, Pauli is said to have commented: "But yes, our friend Dirac has a religion, and the basic postulate of this religion is: 'There is no God, and Dirac is his prophet."

Whatever the authenticity of Heisenberg's story, the gist of it was supported by Dirac's 1933 notes. There, Dirac unambiguously rejected religion as a superstitious belief suitable for only "a primitive community." Any belief in God, he wrote, is "inadmissible from the point of view of modern science ... [and] a well-organized society." Later in life, Dirac expressed some interest in religion, though in his own somewhat naïve and restricted way, he never abandoned his dislike of organized religion.

Dirac may have discussed the relationship between science and religion with his friend Lemaître, the physicist–priest, as he recalled in an insightful memorial article written in 1968. Dirac had first become acquainted with Lemaître in 1933 when the latter gave a talk to the Kapitza Club on his new exploding–universe hypothesis, and they met again in Princeton two years later. In a letter to Margit, Paul Dirac described the Belgian cosmologist as a pleasant man who was "not strictly religious as one might expect from an Abbé." Dirac was pleased with Lemaître's model of an ever-expanding universe, which he thought made room not only for cosmic evolution but also for perpetual biological and human evolution. One might expect, he wrote, that the continuing evolution would lead "to a better and brighter future for all mankind." Dirac suggested to Lemaître that of all the branches of science, cosmology was the one closest to religion:

after all, God supposedly created the universe and the laws governing its structure and evolution. He naturally thought that the eminent cosmologist Lemaître would concur, but "Lemaître did not agree with me. After thinking it over he suggested psychology as lying closest to religion."

A few years later, Dirac discussed in public for the first and only time a religious issue, none other than the existence of God. He insisted on approaching this question, not from the perspective of theology or philosophy—which is "really just sort of guessing or expressing one's feelings"—but from the perspective of physics. In short, Dirac argued that the existence of God was intimately connected with the origin of intelligent life. If life could come into being relatively easily and be explained by the laws of physics, there would be no need for God. On the other hand, "if physical laws are such that to start off life involves an excessively small chance, so that it will not be reasonable to suppose that life would have started just by blind chance, then there must be a god." As usual, Dirac did not commit himself. He did not reveal which of the two possibilities he found the most likely or most appealing.

When it was proposed shortly after Dirac's death to commemorate him in Westminster Abbey, at first, the request was turned down. The reason was not, of course, that the Dean of Westminster doubted Dirac's greatness as a scientist; rather, he questioned, not without reason, whether Dirac had ever been a sincere Christian. Nonetheless, after 11 years of consideration, a commemoration ceremony did take place in the church. Stephen Hawking gave the final address: "It has taken eleven years for the nation to recognise that he was probably the greatest British theoretical physicist since Newton, and belatedly to erect a plaque for him in Westminster Abbey. It is my task to explain why. That is, why he was so great, not why it took so long."

9

Mathematical Beauty

In 1819, the British Romantic poet John Keats composed a poem with the title "Ode on a Greek Urn," which was published six years later. The poem is famous, not least because of its last lines:

> "Beauty is truth, truth beauty—that is all
> Ye know on earth, and all ye need to know."

Keats' enigmatic equation between two apparently unrelated concepts—truth and beauty—has its scientific counterpart in physicists' frequent allusions to beautiful equations. They sometimes state that certain theories or equations are particularly beautiful and *for this reason* supposedly are also fundamental, revealing deep truths about nature. Maxwell's equations of electromagnetism fall into this category. They are fundamental, have a high degree of symmetry and harmony, and they are condensed enough to fit on a T-shirt.

Whatever the meaning of Keats' poem, it is a fact that scientists—and theoretical physicists in particular—often associate their ideas and theories with aesthetic qualities. More than any other modern scientist, Dirac became a prophet of beauty in science, the belief that a truly fundamental theory must be beautiful. But what is beauty? To Dirac, the essential element was one that was missing in Keats' equation (and which Keats probably did not have in mind), namely mathematics. What mattered was not just any kind of beauty, but *mathematical beauty*. Since the mid-1930s, the idea that beautiful mathematics is all-important in fundamental physics had increasingly dominated Dirac's thinking. "A physical law must possess mathematical beauty," Dirac wrote on the blackboard when he visited the University of Moscow in 1956 and was asked to write an inscription summarizing his basic view of physics.

The general idea of an intimate connection between mathematics and physics, sometimes in the more extreme version that nature is, in essence, mathematical, can be found as far back as in ancient Greece. In the early years of the 20th century, it was revived in the form of the influential doctrine of a "pre-established harmony between nature and mathematics," as Hilbert called it. According to Hilbert and his school in Göttingen, the pre-established harmony implied that mathematics was the royal road to progress in theoretical physics. Hilbert and his mathematician colleague, Hermann Minkowski, were deeply involved in the development of the theory of relativity, which they tended to see as a branch of mathematics rather than physics. Max Born and other Göttingen physicists who founded quantum mechanics subscribed happily to Hilbert's doctrine. Most likely Dirac was exposed to a heavy dose of the same doctrine during his visits to Göttingen. By linking it to aesthetical considerations, he developed it in his own way.

In 1960, Eugene Wigner, Dirac's brother-in-law and a former Göttingen student (and Hilbert's assistant), famously discussed the "unreasonable effectiveness of mathematics in the natural sciences." He suggested that the pervasive usefulness of mathematics in physics bordered on the miraculous. This was not a new observation, for in a 1921 lecture Einstein had referred to the same question: "How can it be that mathematics, being after all a product of human thought which is independent of experience, is so admirably appropriate to the objects of reality?" And 18 years later, Dirac repeated: "There is no logical reason why [the method of mathematical reasoning] should be possible at all, but one has found in practice that it does work and meets with considerable success." If there was no logical reason, what reason could there be?

Dirac's answer offered in his 1939 Edinburgh lecture, was that nature possessed a "mathematical quality" or that its fundamental laws were written in the language of mathematics. "One may describe the situation," he explained, "by saying that the mathematician plays a game in which he himself invents the rules while the physicist plays a game in which the rules are provided by Nature, but as time goes on it becomes increasingly evident that the rules which the mathematician finds interesting are the same as those which Nature has chosen." At a later occasion, he phrased the same message in terms similar to those which Galileo had used more than 300 years earlier: "God is a mathematician of a very high order, and he used very advanced mathematics in constructing the universe." Contrary to Galileo, a faithful Catholic, Dirac's rare reference to God was just conventional and not an indication of belief in divine creation. Had Dirac stopped at this point, his idea of a perfect marriage between mathematics and physics would have been rather unoriginal. It would have been just one more version of a line of thought cultivated since antiquity by many other physicists, mathematicians, philosophers, and even theologians.

To claim that nature is constructed in accordance with mathematics, or that the laws of physics are in essence mathematical laws is not very informative. Mathematics is so rich that it can cover almost any imaginable universe (and a good deal more), so why precisely *this* universe? There are immensely more mathematical structures and equations than those which govern the fundamental laws of physics, so why precisely *this* mathematics? The traditional answer, again one with long historical roots, was that nature was constructed in the simplest possible way and therefore described by the simplest possible mathematical structures. *Simplicity* was the answer. Like practically all physicists, Dirac valued simplicity highly, meaning that he preferred simple equations over more complicated ones with the same empirical power. But he thought that simplicity was not enough. Sometimes the endeavor for mathematically simple equations might even lead the researcher astray from the ultimate goal of physics, to find the truths about nature.

In his Edinburgh lecture, Dirac argued that what characterized the deepest and most successful theories of modern physics was *mathematical beauty*, a concept that was not, in general, the same as simplicity. Newton's classical law of gravitation is about as simple as a fundamental law of physics can be, involving only ordinary numbers and simple mathematical operations such as multiplication, division and squaring. On the other hand, Einstein's law, as given by the equations of general relativity, is expressed by a complicated system of equations that involve mathematical quantities called tensors. No doubt Newton's law is simpler than Einstein's; but, Einstein's theory is better, deeper, more general, and nearer to the truth than Newton's. Dirac's advice to his fellow theoretical physicists was to strive towards the element that, more than anything else, characterized Einstein's theory, namely mathematical beauty. "The research worker, in his efforts to express the fundamental laws of Nature in mathematical form, should strive mainly for mathematical beauty," he said. Simplicity was worth considering too but only as subordinate to beauty. "It often happens that the requirements and beauty are the same, but where they clash the latter must take precedence."

Dirac was not always fascinated by mathematical beauty, a concept he first dealt with explicitly and at any length in his Edinburgh address. However, in a more embryonic form, it was in his mind at an earlier date. Without relating specifically to mathematical beauty, in his 1931 paper on the magnetic monopole, he advocated the mathematical route to physical discovery in a way that pointed towards his later, aesthetically formulated view. The surprising physical consequences of his essentially mathematical approach to the electron's wave equation in 1928 were instrumental in turning him into an apostle of mathematically beautiful equations. Although he usually referred to "beauty," sometimes Dirac used other words, which he apparently considered to be synonymous; among them "elegance" and "prettiness." One of his last articles, published on the occasion of his 80th birthday, carried the title "Pretty Mathematics." His favored term for those theories he found to be sorely lacking in beauty was "ugly." Renormalization quantum electrodynamics was his paradigm of a mathematically ugly theory.

Why should the physicist strive toward beautiful mathematics in his equations? Dirac was not aiming at beauty either for artistic or purely mathematical reasons. He was a physicist, neither an artist nor a mathematician, and his main reason for giving such priority to mathematical beauty was that it would lead to better theories of physics. As far as fundamental physics was concerned, he believed that the aesthetic criterion was a safer guide to progress than just agreement with experiment. "A theory with mathematical beauty is more likely to be correct than an ugly one that fits some experimental data," he claimed in 1970, referring to quantum electrodynamics.

For the principle of mathematical beauty to be scientifically valuable, one needs to know more precisely what it is. After all, "beauty" is a nebulous concept and it does not become less nebulous just because "mathematical" is placed in front of it. Dirac was characteristically vague when he spoke, as he often did, on the meaning of mathematical beauty and its role in physical theory. A beautiful theory, he said on one occasion, "is a theory based on simple mathematical concepts that fit together in an elegant way, so that one has pleasure in working with it." Pleasure? Yes, there was an emotional element involved and not just the cold austerity of mathematics and logic. "The beauty of the equations provided by nature … gives one a strong emotional reaction," he stated in a 1979 interview.

The emotional element is also what Dirac indicated in a moving obituary he wrote for his friend and colleague Schrödinger in 1961. He confided that the Austrian physicist was "the one that I felt to be most closely similar to myself." The reason, he believed, was that "Schrödinger and I both had a very strong appreciation of mathematical beauty, and this appreciation of mathematical beauty dominated all our work." Dirac described it "as a sort of faith with us that any equations which describe fundamental laws of nature must have great beauty in them. It was like a religious faith with us."

There is little doubt that Dirac relied on his own intuitions and basic beliefs, and also on his personal experiences as a physicist when he decided which mathematical methods and concepts were beautiful and which were ugly. Nonetheless, he suggested that his own intuitions were largely the same as those of other mathematicians and physicists. "Mathematical beauty," he wrote, "is a quality which cannot be defined, any more than beauty in art can be defined, but which people who study mathematics usually have no difficulty in appreciating." And yet, contrary to the subjective nature of beauty in painting, sculpture, poetry and theater, he believed that mathematical beauty was objective and absolute, almost as it existed in a Platonic heaven. This is what Dirac said in a talk given in Florida in 1972. "It is of a completely different kind. It is the same in all countries and at all periods of time." No justification was given, and no further explication followed.

What if a mathematically beautiful theory flatly disagrees with evidence from experiment and observation? This happened to Dirac's theory of a varying gravitational constant based on the beautiful hypothesis of interconnected constants of nature. Aware of the dilemma, Dirac proposed the radical idea that in some cases considerations of mathematical aesthetics should be given greater weight than experimental facts. In effect, the principle of mathematical beauty would then become a criterion of truth, overruling the traditional criterion of experimental testing. Dirac spelled out his radical proposal in no uncertain terms: "There are occasions when mathematical beauty should take priority over agreement with experiment."

Just as Dirac believed that a beautiful theory should not be rejected just because it contradicted experiments, so he believed that empirically successful theories might nonetheless be wrong if they were aesthetically displeasing. Empirical virtues and aesthetic shortcomings may well go together, as was the case with the "ugly and incomplete" theory of quantum electrodynamics. In Dirac's view, aesthetic criteria could and in some cases should preserve a theory from refutation in the face of falsifying experiments; the same criteria could also prompt the abandonment, or at least mistrust of, a theory that is as yet empirically satisfactory.

Did Dirac seriously mean that the physicist, convinced of the sublime beauty of some theory, should obstinately stick to that theory and disregard any kind of conflicting evidence, however strong? Not really, for Dirac realized that, in the long run, a scientist could not ignore the verdict of experiment and still be credible as a scientist. What he did mean and was quite serious about, was that the physicist should not care *too much* if a beautiful theory were *apparently* disproved by experiments. He liked to illustrate the point by referring to Einstein's admired theory of general relativity. Let us imagine that a discrepancy, well confirmed and substantiated, had turned up shortly after Einstein had completed his theory. Should one then conclude that the theory had been falsified, or proved wrong? Not according to Dirac and also, for that matter, not according to Einstein. "Anyone who appreciates the fundamental harmony connecting the way nature runs and general mathematical principles must feel that a theory with the beauty and elegance of Einstein's theory *has* to be substantially correct," Dirac stated.

Apart from Einstein and general relativity, Dirac often referred to Heisenberg's original quantum mechanics as a beautiful theory, despite its lack of incorporating relativity. Remarkably, he never discussed his own contributions in this context. Many physicists of today would single out Dirac's linear wave equation of 1928 as a masterpiece of beauty, harmony, and elegance, but Dirac never mentioned it. He was too modest to call attention to his own work.

10

Dirac's Legacy

Paul Adrien Maurice Dirac was a legend in his own lifetime, and his status in the history of recent physics has not diminished since his death. He died on October 20, 1984, in Florida and was buried at Roselawn Cemetery in Tallahassee. Shortly after his death, the Institute of Physics, the organization for physicists in the United Kingdom of which Dirac had been an Honorary Fellow since 1971, established the Paul Dirac Medal, to be awarded annually to outstanding contributors to physics. The first recipient was the famous astrophysicist and expert in general relativity Stephen Hawking, who at the time occupied the Lucasian Chair formerly held by Dirac. Another Dirac Medal was established by the Abdus Salam International Centre for Theoretical Physics located in Trieste, Italy. The publishing branch of the Institute of Physics is located in the Dirac House in his native Bristol, where one can also find the small and unimpressive Dirac Road. In 1989, The Paul A. M. Dirac Science Library was inaugurated at Florida State University, containing, among other items, Dirac's papers and archival materials related to his life and career.

Dirac did not invent quantum mechanics, but together with Heisenberg, Born, Jordan and Pauli, he belonged to the small group of highly talented physicists who originally established the theory. Much of Dirac's early work in the area was independent of the work done by his German colleagues and friendly competitors, yet his breakthrough in the fall of 1925 relied crucially on Heisenberg's original insight. Would Dirac have made inroads in quantum mechanics without Heisenberg's paper? It is impossible to say, but probably not. In any case, Dirac always acknowledged Heisenberg as the founder of quantum mechanics and never claimed priority either to this field or other theoretical discoveries. Priority claims were just not his style.

Dirac's name is first of all associated with the Dirac equation, the relativistic wave equation for the electron, which he had ready in January 1928 and which had a galvanizing effect on theoretical physics—leading to the idea of antimatter, and much more. Connected to the wave equation are names such as Dirac operators, Dirac matrices, and Dirac measure, which are familiar not only to physicists but, perhaps even more so, to mathematicians. Even before the emergence of the Dirac wave equation, the name of the young British physicist was turned into an eponymy in the Dirac delta function and in the Fermi-Dirac quantum statistics characterizing the electron and many other elementary particles. While Dirac operators and Fermi-Dirac statistics are accepted and semi-official names, the "dirac" unit is mostly anecdotal and based on the physicist's succinct manner. It is a measure of taciturnity or slowness of speech, the smallest number of words used in a conversation. Its exact value is unknown but, according to some experts, one dirac corresponds to one word per hour.

The "Dirac-Kapitza effect" may be little known, but it is not without either scientific or historical interest. An arch-theorist with a predilection for mathematical theories and fundamental physics, Dirac at times descended from his theoretical heaven to more mundane experimental problems. Collaborating with Kapitza, an experimental physicist, in 1933, he discussed the possibility of obtaining electron diffraction from a grating of standing light waves. Given the wave-particle dualism of quantum mechanics, such an effect—the opposite of the ordinary diffraction of light in a material grating—should be at least theoretically possible. Dirac and Kapitza calculated the probability and obtained a ridiculously small number, which suggested that the effect was outside the reach of an experiment. Not very much more happened until 1986, when both physicists had passed away. In that year, physicists at the Massachusetts Institute of Technology succeeded in detecting the phenomenon predicted by Dirac and Kapitza 53 years earlier, albeit using sodium atoms instead of electrons. Two years later, the diffraction of electrons by standing light waves was demonstrated. Today the Dirac-Kapitza effect (sometimes referred to as the Kapitza-Dirac effect) is well known and a thriving field of research in the community of condensed matter physics.

While Dirac had a tremendous influence on scientific thought, his impact on British science and science education was much more limited. Considering that Dirac was at Cambridge University for 47 years, of which he spent 37 years as a Lucasian professor, his local influence may be said to have been very small. His taciturn and reticent nature was part of the reason, and so was his dislike of public appearances. Dirac tried hard and largely successfully to stay out of the public limelight, not to be part of committees, and not to take on administrative duties. He was totally uninterested in exerting power or influence of any kind. The idea of building up a school of physics, something equivalent to what Rutherford and Bohr had done, probably never crossed his mind. Although he was pleased to be appointed as a Lucasian professor, the position itself did not seem to have interested him very much. More than once he was compared to Newton, but the comparison did not impress him. Nor did he pay any attention to the history of the Lucasian chair or to his illustrious predecessors, including not only Newton, but also Gabriel Stokes, Joseph Larmor, and other important physicists. In his letters to colleagues from 1932 and 1933, he did not even mention the new position or commented about being Lucasian professor in his later writings and correspondence.

The broader impact Dirac did have was primarily through his lectures on quantum mechanics and his textbook on which the lectures were always based. Physicists following his course have hailed Dirac's "exceptionally clear" presentation, noting that the audience "was carried along in the unfolding of an argument which seemed as majestic and inevitable as the development of a Bach fugue." Dirac's lectures were indeed clear and well structured, but for three decades they largely followed the same pattern as outlined in his textbook, which he considered to be *the* way of presenting quantum mechanics. He delivered his lectures tersely and with little interaction with his audience. If the students did not understand him, they could not expect much help. One can safely assume that not all students appreciated Dirac's lucid and majestic arguments. Some might have wished to listen to a Liszt rhapsody or even a folk song rather than a Bach fugue. Dirac had only a few Ph.D. students and was, in general, uninterested in them; in fact, he expected the students to work largely on their own. The German–American physicist Victor Weisskopf called him "absolutely unusable for any student." It is probably correct to say that, although Dirac's physics was a model of inspiration, Dirac himself was not a role model for any of his students. But then, he had no intention of being a role model.

Dirac's life can be divided into four phases, the first being his youth and early training in Bristol. Only when he arrived in Cambridge in 1923 did his genius unfold, and two years later he entered the avant-garde of international theoretical physics. During the next decade or so, the second phase, he produced a phenomenal record of innovative ideas and theories that forever changed the physical world picture. All of these ideas and theories were concerned with quantum mechanics. This second phase of his life was far the most significant from the perspective of science, the theory of antiparticles perhaps being the deepest, most original, and most astounding of all his contributions. Not only was the substance of his work unique, but the way he presented his discoveries to the world of science was also in a style rarely, if ever, seen before. The British-American mathematical physicist Freeman Dyson, one of the chief architects of the new quantum electrodynamics, wrote about Dirac's explosion of creativity: "His great discoveries were like exquisitely carved marble statues falling out of the sky, one after another. He seemed to be able to conjure laws of nature from pure thought—it was this purity that made him unique."

Had Dirac died in 1936, perhaps fallen from one of the summits he climbed so eagerly, it would not have mattered much to his legacy in physics. During the third and longest phase of his life, Dirac, now married, continued doing important work in quantum theory but not of the same quality and innovative nature as previously. There were gems here and there, but fewer and less precious. Dissatisfied with the new trends in theoretical physics in general and with renormalization quantum electrodynamics, in particular, after World War II Dirac increasingly distanced himself from mainstream physics. His long and lonely fight against the infinite quantities appearing in quantum theory was the fight of a loser. Dirac more or less knew it, but he just fought on. For a period, he switched to problems of general relativity, a line of work he enjoyed and which was appreciated by contemporary physicists. Yet, the foundation of quantum mechanics was constantly on his mind.

At the age of 67, Dirac was forced to retire from his chair in Cambridge, much to his regret. He was upset that the university did not want to give him even the space of the small room he occupied at Cambridge. Although he felt marginalized and was dissatisfied with the modernization of the university's organization, he wanted to go on as usual. He spent the fourth and last phase of his life in Florida. In 1968, he had been invited to visit the Center for Theoretical Studies at the University of Miami and three years later he joined the physics department at Florida State University, Tallahassee. He remained scientifically active and continued his project of reformulating quantum mechanics into a logically more satisfactory theory. However, Dirac's main occupation during the Florida period was cosmology rather than quantum theory. The project to establish a new cosmological theory based on the hypothesis of a varying gravitational constant was a resurrection of the idea he had introduced as early as 1937. It was even less mainstream than his work in quantum mechanics. Although attracting some interest among physicists, geologists, and astronomers, observations consistently disagreed with the predictions of Dirac's gravitation hypothesis.

When Dirac is commemorated as one of the greatest physicists ever, it is mainly because of his epoch-making contributions to quantum physics made in the second phase of his life. Given the outstanding quality of these contributions, it is only natural that he was unable to reach the same level of successful creativity later in life. After all, and despite his reputation, Dirac was only a human. Even Einstein's career was divided into a highly creative early phase and much less productive later years. At the end of his life, Dirac felt that his earlier successes did not quite make up for his later failures. In 1983, he was addressed by Pierre Ramond, then a 40-year-old Florida theoretical physicist known for his important work in string theory. Ramond sought to engage the famous physicist in a conversation, but Dirac evaded: "I have nothing to talk about. My life has been a failure." One understands Ramond's surprise and even shock: "I could hardly believe that such a great man could look back on his life as a failure," he noted. "What did that say about the rest of us?"

Suggested Reading

Not very much has been written about Dirac and there is even less material that is accessible to the general reader. This is perhaps understandable, given Dirac's reclusive nature, his lack of involvement in politics, culture, and social life, and his highly abstract contributions to fundamental physics. All the same, there are sources that illuminate not only his works in physics, but also his life and thoughts more generally. Two of these sources stand out as the only full-scale biographical memoirs. The one by Helge Kragh titled *Dirac: A Scientific Biography* (1990) integrates Dirac's life and his many contributions to the physical sciences, including the philosophical views of this most unphilosophical scientist. On the other hand, Graham Farmelo's 2009 book, *The Strangest Man*, pays relatively little attention to Dirac's physics, but describes very richly and innovatively his personality and relations to family and friends. While these two books are far the most detailed and informative sources about Dirac, it is still worth consulting some of the physicists' own writings, which appeared shortly after his death. Richard Henry Dalitz and Rudolf Ernst Peierls, two distinguished physicists who knew Dirac well, wrote, in 1986, an authoritative and non-technical account of Dirac's life and career, Paul Adrian Maurice Dirac, *Biographical Memoirs of Fellows of the Royal Society*. Another interesting and readable account appears in a chapter in Abraham Pais' 2000 work, *The Genius of Science: A Portrait Gallery*. Kursunoglu and Eugene Wigner (1987) as well as John Taylor (1987), wrote memorial anthologies that contain a mixture of physics and biography, including many of the anecdotes told about Dirac (see index below). Peter Goddard's 1998 book, *Paul Dirac: The Man and his Work,* is yet another example of this genre, which is addressed primarily to physicists.

While most of the scientifically oriented literature on Dirac focuses on his work in quantum theory, Kragh's book mentioned above pays attention to his unorthodox cosmological theory based on the assumption of varying gravity. This subject is also covered in Kragh's 2015 fictional interview, *Masters of the Universe: Conversations with Cosmologists of the Past.*

Sources:

Bernstein, Jeremy (2009). "P. A. M. Dirac: Some strangeness in the proportion," *American Journal of Physics* 77, 979-987.

Berry, Michael (1998). "Paul Dirac: The purest soul in physics," *Physics World* 11 (February), 36-40.

Brian, Denis (1995). *The Voice of Genius: Conversations with Nobel Scientists and other Luminaries*. Cambridge, MA: Perseus Publishing.

Buckley, Paul and F. David Peat (1979). *A Question of Physics: Conversations in Physics and Biology*. London: Routledge & Kegan Paul.

Dalitz, Richard H. and Rudolf Peierls (1986). "Paul Adrian Maurice Dirac," *Biographical Memoirs of Fellows of the Royal Society* 32, 139-185.

Farmelo, Graham (2009). *The Strangest Man: The Hidden Life of Paul Dirac, Quantum Genius*. London: Faber and Faber.

Galison, Peter (2000). "The suppressed drawings: Paul Dirac's hidden geometry," *Representations* 72, 145-166.

Goddard, Peter, ed. (1998). *Paul Dirac: The Man and his Work*. Cambridge: Cambridge University Press.

Hovis, R. Corby and Helge Kragh (1993)."P. A. M. Dirac and the beauty of physics," *Scientific American* 268 (May), 104-109.

Kragh, Helge (1990). *Dirac: A Scientific Biography*. Cambridge: Cambridge University Press.

Kragh, Helge (2002). "Paul Dirac: Seeking beauty," *Physics World* 15 (August), 27-31.

Kragh, Helge (2013). "Paul Dirac and The Principles of Quantum Mechanics," pp. 225-238 in *Research and Pedagogy: A History of Quantum Physics through its Textbooks*, M. Badino and J. Navarro, Eds. Berlin: Edition Open Access.

Kragh, Helge (2015). *Masters of the Universe: Conversations with Cosmologists of the Past*. Oxford: Oxford University Press.

Kursunoglu, Behram N. and Eugene P. Wigner, eds. (1987). *Paul Adrien Maurice Dirac: Reminiscences about a Great Physicist*. Cambridge: Cambridge University Press.

McAllister, James W. (1990). "Dirac and the aesthetic evaluation of theories," *Methodology and Science* 23, 87-102.

Pais, Abraham (2000). *The Genius of Science: A Portrait Gallery*. Oxford: Oxford University Press.

Taylor, John G., ed. (1987). *Tributes to Paul Dirac*. Bristol: Adam Hilger.

About the Author

Emeritus Professor at the Niels Bohr Institute in Copenhagen, **Helge Kragh** is the author of numerous books on physics and cosmology, including the first full-length biography of Paul Dirac, *Dirac: A Scientific Biography*. Among his other books are *Cosmology and Controversy* (1999), *Quantum Generations: A History of Physics in the Twentieth Century* (2002), and *Conceptions of Cosmos* (2013).

Afterword

Thank you for reading *Simply Dirac*!

If you enjoyed reading it, we would be grateful if you could help others discover and enjoy it too.

Please review it with your favorite book provider such as Amazon, BN, Kobo, iBook and Goodreads, among others.

Again, thank you for your support and we look forward to offering you more great reads in the future.

A Note on the Type

Cardo is an Old Style font specifically designed for the needs of classicists, Biblical scholars, medievalists, and linguists. Created by David J. Perry, it was inspired by a typeface cut for the Renaissance printer Aldus Manutius that he first used to print Pietro Bembo's book *De Aetna*, which has been revived in modern times under several names.